Promoting Transborder Dialogue During Times of Uncertainty

Promoting Transborder Dialogue During Times of Uncertainty

A Time for Third Spaces

Timothy G. Cashman

LEXINGTON BOOKS
Lanham • Boulder • New York • London

Published by Lexington Books
An imprint of The Rowman & Littlefield Publishing Group, Inc.
4501 Forbes Boulevard, Suite 200, Lanham, Maryland 20706
www.rowman.com

6 Tinworth Street, London SE11 5AL, United Kingdom

Copyright © 2021 by The Rowman & Littlefield Publishing Group, Inc.

All rights reserved. No part of this book may be reproduced in any form or by any electronic or mechanical means, including information storage and retrieval systems, without written permission from the publisher, except by a reviewer who may quote passages in a review.

British Library Cataloguing in Publication Information Available

Library of Congress Cataloging-in-Publication Data

Names: Cashman, Timothy G., author.
Title: Promoting transborder dialogue during times of uncertainty : a time for third spaces / Timothy G. Cashman.
Description: Lanham : Lexington Books, [2021] | Includes bibliographical references and index. | Summary: "This book explicates the process of critical border praxis and establishes the need for dialogic border crossings. It also articulates how the creation and development of third spaces allow for the convergence of transborder negotiations within educational and political spheres"—Provided by publisher.
Identifiers: LCCN 2021021285 (print) | LCCN 2021021286 (ebook) | ISBN 9781793600219 (cloth) | ISBN 9781793600226 (ebook) | ISBN 9781793600233 (pbk)
Subjects: LCSH: Critical pedagogy—Cross-cultural studies. | Transborder ethnic groups—Social conditions—Cross-cultural studies. | Border crossing—Cross-cultural studies. | Intercultural communication—Cross-cultural studies.
Classification: LCC LC196 .C39 2021 (print) | LCC LC196 (ebook) | DDC 370.11/5—dc23
LC record available at https://lccn.loc.gov/2021021285
LC ebook record available at https://lccn.loc.gov/2021021286

Contents

List of Figures and Tables		vii
Acknowledgments		ix
1	Introduction	1
2	Border Pedagogy Revisited	7
3	An Examination of Place-Based Pedagogies	17
4	Transborder Dialogue: Intersections of Meliorism, Heteroglossia, Nepantla, and Dialogic Feminism	29
5	Transnational Possibilities: The Importance of Critical Cosmopolitanism and Pragmatic Hope	43
6	Navigating the Intersection of Border Pedagogy and Critical Place-Based Pedagogies	49
7	Critical Border Praxis: Choosing the Path	63
8	Transnational Educational Research in Four Countries: Examples of Critical Border Praxis	73
9	"In Spite of the Way the World Is": What U.S. Educators Can Learn from Their Counterparts in Cuba	87
10	"They Did Not Make Their Decisions on a Whim": Teaching Border Issues on the United States and Mexico Border	103
11	In Pursuit of Comparative Pedagogies	119

| **12** | Emergent Third Spaces | 131 |
| **13** | Conclusion: There Has Never Been a More Crucial Time | 141 |

Works Cited — 153

Index — 165

About the Author — 169

List of Figures and Tables

FIGURES

Figure 6.1	Theoretical Underpinnings of a Critical Border Dialogism	61
Figure 8.1	Components of Critical Border Praxis	85

TABLES

Table 9.1	Components of Critical Border Dialogism and Critical Border Praxis	92
Table 9.2	Critical Border Praxis and Lessons Learned from Cuban Educators	101
Table 10.1	Traits of Participants	107

Acknowledgments

I would like to thank all those who have agreed to participate in my research projects to date. My efforts could not have been completed without the cooperation of supportive educators, including school administrators. My sincerest gratitude is extended to all of those who have agreed to participate and provide assistance for my investigations.

Most importantly, I choose to recognize my parents, who played such vital roles in my educational development. In particular, this book is dedicated to my mother, Donna Hughes Cashman, a former educator herself and a driving influence for my scholarship.

Chapter 1

Introduction

BACKGROUND

Promoting Border Dialogue During Times of Uncertainty: A Time for Third Spaces is the product of years of investigations and publications focusing on the importance of dialogic processes in the fields of education, cultural work, economics, and politics. Recent, pivotal events make all the more pressing the need for reimagining, reconceptualizing, redesigning, and reconstructing educational and governmental institutions. Given the extent to which current educational and governmental policies are shaping discourses, hope for the amelioration of racial-, ethnic-, class-, religion-, and gender-based conflicts resides in the implementation of effective dialogue. This dialogue must cross borders, internally and externally. Border crossings, not limited to geographic or political, are requisite for understandings of the current local, regional, national, transnational, and global conditions.

The upcoming book explores numerous key theoretical constructs, as put forth in the following chapters. Additionally, the implications of recent events for critical praxis and the creation of third spaces will be noted. Recent events in the United States and worldwide add the urgency of addressing and responding to existential issues confronting educational institutions, societies, economies, and governments at all levels. In less than four months, populations worldwide have been forced to face the realities of COVID-19 pandemic, unlike any previous worldwide adversity. Couple the ongoing pandemic with worldwide movements to counter systemic racism, social inequities, and social injustices, and White privilege, and what is being experienced on a global scale has no precise precedent. Those tremors are being felt no more strongly elsewhere than the United States as disinformation, political tensions, incendiary tweets, and carefully orchestrated distractions preoccupy a nation with uncertainty. However, we must remain steadfast in a pragmatic hope that is grounded in ongoing struggles and provides pathways to meliorism, faith, and social progress (Shade, 2001; Stitzlein, 2019). For pragmatic hope to become fruition, however, we must collectively acknowledge and engage in democratic and dialogic processes that promote participation, experiences, and agency.

When I first began work on cross-border studies the warning signs for one-dimensional and/or dualistic education and government policies were clearly evident. In March 2003, the United States and its allies commenced the bombing of Baghdad, Iraq, under the completely discredited and now-disavowed guise of Saddam Hussein's "weapons of mass destruction." This would signal the commencement of the Iraq military invasion and government takeover.

At the time of these events, I was visiting in-laws in Sabah, Malaysia. I observed the coverage on Al Jazeera television network of women and children being carried out of destroyed buildings on stretchers or completely covered in sheets. I also noticed how major international television news sources, including CNN and the BBC were self-censoring such images. This led to the question of "I wonder how educators in this part of Malaysia are addressing the (already commenced) US-led War in Iraq?"

In the year that followed I made a return trip to Sabah to interview educators of various backgrounds in diverse school settings. I followed on this initial investigation with studies of how teachers taught of U.S. transnational policies, including anti-terrorism and wars, in eastern Ontario, Canada; Chihuahua, Mexico; and on the U.S. side of the US/Mexico. I researched how teachers led discourses as a part of their curricula or as a part of focused teacher-facilitated extraneous classroom discussions. The findings of these studies, and additional research, were included in *Developing a Critical Border Dialogism: Learning from Fellow Educators in Malaysia, Mexico, Canada, and the United States.*

This book follows on published works, including border pedagogy, critical place-based pedagogies and considers heteroglossia, meliorism, nepantla, critical cosmopolitanism, dialogic feminism, and pragmatic hope as the basis for putting theoretical constructs into educational practice, or critical border praxis. *Developing a Critical Border Dialogism: Learning from Fellow Educators in Malaysia, Mexico, Canada, and the United States* (Cashman, 2015) addressed the importance of critical cross-border dialogue in educational settings. *Promoting Border Dialogue During Times of Uncertainty: A Time for Third Spaces,* on the other hand, elucidates how critical border praxis, based on Gramsci's interpretation of praxis, can function in our society and educational systems, given our current educational and political environments. This book continues to explore U.S.

transborder issues and also other comparative, transnational educational, economic, historical, political, and societal concerns. Thus, this latest effort serves to clarify and contextualize how critical border praxis plays out in contemporary contexts.

Border studies examine borders as diverse socio-spatial and geographic scales (Kolossov & Scott, 2013). Transnational studies promote comparisons and further discourses and dialogue on the importance of border crossings in the field of education. Giroux (2005) contemplated both the limits and possibilities of border crossings. Borders, in broader contexts, also represent limitations to our present understandings of society, including what sorts of limitations exist in our educational institutions.

Perceptions change when individuals engage in empirical research and educate across borders. According to Gramsci (1971), praxis involves the enactment, embodiment, or realization of a theory, lesson, or skill. Critical border praxis situates theory in practice and engages students, educators, cultural workers, and policy makers in transborder reasoning for the common good. Critical border praxis (Cashman, 2015, 2016a, 2016b) follows on the tenets of heteroglossia, meliorism, nepantla, dialogic feminism, critical cosmopolitanism, and pragmatic hope to provide possibilities for education that values human potential and sustainability.

Highly influential to this book are the earlier scholarly contributions of such individuals as Bakhtin, Gramsci, Dewey, Freire, Bowles and Gintis, Giroux, Anzaldúa, and Gruenewald. Chapters 2 through 6 build upon concepts explored in *Developing a Critical Border Dialogism: Learning from Fellow Educators in Malaysia, Mexico, Canada, and the United States* while further explicating theoretical constructs that form a rationale for critical border praxis. The remaining chapters of *Promoting Border Dialogue During Times of Uncertainty: A Time for Third Spaces* (chapters 7 through 15) explore the possibilities for critical border praxis, including recent research applications of cross-border investigations. As such, a breakdown for the book chapters reads as follows:

Chapter 2 revisits and rethinks border pedagogy. Cross-border understandings are necessary at a time when the current federal government has promoted public pedagogies of hate that encourages his supporters and potential supporters to blame all of the nation's shortcomings and problems on Latinx, Muslims, Native-Americans, African-Americans, immigrants, and anti-fascists. According to Cole (2019), anti-intellectual and anti-science posturing and policies of the Trump administration reiterate a right-wing public pedagogy for fascism. Since 2016, the alt-right and Trump administration have promoted the construction of a White ethno-state (Cole, 2019), which effectively disregards border crossings and discourages efficacious transborder communications and transactions. On the contrary, border pedagogy seeks to develop democratic public philosophy that recognizes and respects difference as part of human interactions. Within border pedagogy educators engage in political processes of revitalizing institutions and perspectives.

Chapter 3 examines critical place-based pedagogies. Conceptualizations of place are central to the contemplation of borders, spatial interactions, and transborder education. Place-based education promotes and engages students with their communities, including educational institutions. Place-based education, as a process, incorporates the local environs as a focal point in an integrated curriculum. Students participate in hands-on, project-based learning experiences with goals of improving academic achievement. Learning demonstrates an appreciation for the natural surroundings, as well as the human development of critical, reasoning, and logical contributors to society.

Chapter 4 addresses the intersections of meliorism, heteroglossia, nepantla, and dialogic feminism. The chapter examines how effective cross-border dialogue intersects with the concepts and theoretical constructs related to meliorism, heteroglossia, nepantla, and dialogic feminism. Accordingly, meliorism maps out strategies for unfettered advancement of the human condition.

Bakhtin (1981) refers to heteroglossia as the consideration and realization of language as exemplary of one's values, conceptualizations, and experiences. It reveals varied, personal perspectives and epistemology. Nepantla, according to Anzaldua's view, is time where individuals experience a loss of control and suffer anxiety and confusion as a result. The term was employed by Nahuatl-speaking people in Mexico during the sixteenth century. During this time, they were being colonized by Spaniards and the concept of being "in between" was useful to describe how the experience felt (Mignolo, 2000). According to Anzaldúa (1987), nepantla is a space where multiple forms of reality are viewed simultaneously. Thus, the process of nepantla involves coming to terms with seemingly competing concepts. Nepantla offers possibilities for the promotion of new and original concepts as an outgrowth of conflicts. Dialogic feminism furthers dialogue with regard to common struggles among women of divergent backgrounds. Moreover, new inclusive spaces are created for discourses among non-academic women, immigrant women, or women from ethnic minorities together with women in academia. In this manner, shortcomings of the current women's movement are addressed so that women are empowered to confront and challenge societal injustices and inequities.

Chapter 5 elaborates on views of critical cosmopolitanism and pragmatic hope as key components of productive transborder dialogue. Discourses across geographic, socioeconomic, historical, and psychological borders are contingent on critical cosmopolitanism and, ultimately, pragmatic hope. Critical cosmopolitanism differs from normative accounts of cosmopolitanism as it emphasizes internal developmental processes rather than globalization as the foremost factor in cosmopolitanism. Thus, critical cosmopolitanism is a post-universalistic form of cosmopolitanism. Pragmatic hope complements critical cosmopolitanism by addressing problematic conditions that preclude hopeful aspirations. A key component of pragmatic hope is that it functions to provide possible resolutions for problems.

Chapter 6 is entitled "Navigating the Intersection of Border Pedagogy and Critical Place-Based Pedagogies." This chapter explicates the intersection of place-based and border pedagogies, including how transnational, comparative studies and issues-centered pedagogies are central to understanding one's own situatedness and positions. Place-based and border pedagogies provide a platform for effectively crossing borders inherent to larger research, intellectual knowledge, appreciation, and learning. Critical border dialogism engages educators, cultural workers, and policy makers in a multiplicity of discourses and interchange that follows on the concepts of heteroglossia, meliorism, critical cosmopolitanism, nepantla, dialogic feminism, and pragmatic hope.

Chapter 7 articulates the importance of choosing and following a path of critical border praxis. The chapter explicates how the intersectionalities of heteroglossia, meliorism, critical cosmopolitanism, nepantla, dialogic feminism, and pragmatic hope comprise essential components of transborder dialogue and efficacious border crossings. Critical border praxis draws upon a critical pedagogy of place and border pedagogy and actively engages us as border crossers who challenge historically, socially, politically, and economically constructed liminal spaces.

Chapter 8 provides a cross-comparative analysis of previous research conducted in four countries—Malaysia, Mexico, Canada, and the United States. Critical border praxis served as the theoretical construct emergent across the transnational studies. For this chapter, input from educators in the four selected countries revealed how U.S. transnational policies were addressed with the curricula of those nations. This chapter includes recommendations for how U.S. social studies educators can include and address the impact of U.S. international rhetoric, decisions, and policies.

Chapter 9 takes into account the findings of research conducted with Cuban educators as part of a transnational educator exchange. This study underscores the importance of cross-border dialogue in Cuban and the United States in educational exchanges. The research provides insights into how selected educators facilitate discourses on current and historical Cuban and U.S. relations. The investigation articulates the need for emergent third spaces for Cuban and U.S. relations, including future educational collaborations and exchanges.

Chapter 10 includes a case study of how educators on the U.S. side of the U.S./Mexico border address border issues, including immigration. The chapter emphasizes the importance of teaching issues surrounding immigration and the mistreatment of refugees, including children. With ever-changing U.S. governmental policies and social upheaval, immigration issues have receded from the media and national spotlight. The current plight of immigrants, many of whom are refugees, in subhuman conditions and the root causes for their immigration are disregarded. Thus, this chapter reveals how immigration issues and U.S. transnational policies are addressed in upper elementary classrooms on the U.S./Mexico border.

Chapter 11, "In Pursuit of Comparative Pedagogies," addresses what sort of agency is needed, as well as a current urgency, for critical border praxis. Dialogic teaching and transborder thinking dialogue encourage, facilitate, question, and broadens student communications. Border praxis in educational settings, in turn, is comprised of interactive modes within classrooms, everyday types of classroom discourses, creative ways of promoting classroom learning, motivational language, questioning strategies, and extension activities.

Chapter 12 articulates the possibilities for "Emergent Third Spaces." A current preeminent concern of educators, cultural workers, and policy makers is how to resolve seemingly insurmountable disunity within society. Meaningful and enduring conflict resolution requires effective dialogic processes. New, emergent third spaces that consider the common good rather than self-serving mandates of those in power, regardless of political party affiliation. These developments must counter prevailing populist sentiments that view undemocratic and authoritarian rhetoric as an antidote to personal shortcomings and fears.

Chapter 13 serves as the concluding chapter of *Promoting Transborder Dialogue During Times of Uncertainty: A Time for Third Spaces.* Key positions, as put forth in previous chapters, will be revisited. This chapter also explicates how recent events have reinforced a need for critical praxis and the creation of third spaces. The conclusion also questions and speculates on the possibilities for efficacious, reasoned deliberations within local, national, and world forums. Recommendations are offered for present and future deliberations and conflict resolution within educational, social, economic, and political settings.

Chapter 2

Border Pedagogy Revisited

INTRODUCTION

My most recent research has been carried out with educators on the U.S. side of the U.S./Mexico border. That research uncovered how teachers and administrators perceive local issues, including immigration fears, are being discussed in sixth grade classrooms. Border pedagogy has served as a framework for the data analyses of interviews and formal observations conducted with educators in this study, as well as previous research conducted in Malaysia, Mexico, Canada, and Cuba.

Overview of Border Pedagogy

Given recent events of recent years and months, including the ongoing COVID-19 virus pandemic, changes in immigration and border policies following the outcome of the U.S. national election of 2016, and political party stances leading up to the 2020 general elections, cross-border dialogue has been replaced with unilateral policy making. Inflammatory rhetoric from a sitting U.S. president, coupled with acts of violence in Charlottesville, Virginia, underscored a new reality for border residents and U.S. citizens of color throughout the country (CBS News/AP, 2019). With regards to the U.S. and Mexico border, a mass shooting took place during August of 2019 in El Paso, Texas, with twenty-three border residents killed and twenty-four injured in the allegedly pre-meditated attack. The perpetrator, by his own account, was motivated by the president's anti-immigration rhetoric and drove more than 10 hours from another part of Texas just to slaughter "as many Mexicans," in his own words as possible.

If ever there were a time for increased cross-border understandings augmented by and through border pedagogy, it most certainly is the present. In particular, rhetoric during the Trump administration promoted a public pedagogy of xenophobia that encouraged supporters and potential supporters to blame all of the nation's shortcomings and problems on Latinx, Muslims, Native-Americans, African-Americans, Haitians, and anti-fascists. According to Cole (2019), anti-intellectual and anti-science posturing and policies of the Trump administration encouraged a right-wing pedagogy of hate. After Donald Trump's election in 2016, the alt-right and the presidential administration promoted the construction of a white ethno-state (Cole, 2019).

The general concept behind border pedagogy is to develop a "democratic public philosophy that respects the notion of difference as part of a common struggle to extend the quality of public life" (Giroux, 2005, p. 20). Border pedagogy is political in the process of rehabilitating historical and ideological institutions and considering the narratives of those who have been historically and culturally excluded. In this respect, educators become cultural workers (Kazanjian, 2011).

Border pedagogy (Garza, 2007; Giroux, 1992, 2005; Ramirez et al., 2016; Salinas et al., 2016) is an approach utilized by teachers to disrupt the manner in which students are being educated in high schools. Border pedagogy teaches the skills of critical thinking and debating power, meaning, and identity. Border pedagogy works to revitalize learning and teaching to promote justice for all (Giroux, 1992; Romo & Chavez, 2006). Giroux (1992) affirmed that border pedagogy is fundamental approach used to engage youth in becoming social critics of their realities. Border pedagogy allows the student to learn how borders have served to perpetuate power and difference (Kasanjian, 2011). Once one acknowledges these constructed boundaries, one is able to step outside them. Perspectives developed from the margins "students and educators are able to critically deconstruct the narratives, knowledges, and languages that have shaped their histories and experiences" Kasanjian (2011, p. 373). Giroux (2005) maintains students must not only learn to cross borders but also redefine the borders and otherness with which they felt they were familiar. Through understandings of the historical and social apparatuses of border students better understand limitations and qualifications. Border pedagogy also teaches students to question how own personal experiences are defined.

The importance of border pedagogy lies in its value as a counter-narrative to unilateral or dualistic, point/counterpoint perspectives. Participants engage with multiple cultural codes, experiences, and languages as part of their roles within border pedagogy (Giroux, 1988). Through this approach, codified descriptions are critiqued, and limitations are challenged. When we examine the world through the lenses of border pedagogy we are invited to deconstruct and reconstruct our own personal histories and experiences, as well as traditional storylines. Thus, authoritative discourses are challenged when individuals become border crossers. According to Giroux (1988), there are not only physical borders but also

> cultural borders historically constructed and socially organized within maps of rules and regulations that limit and enable particular identities, individual capacities, and social forms. In this case, students cross over into borders of meaning, maps of knowledge, social relations, and values that are increasingly being negotiated and rewritten as the codes and regulations which organize them become destabilized and reshaped. Border pedagogy decenters as it remaps. The terrain of learning becomes inextricably linked to the shifting parameters of place, identity, history, and power. (p. 166)

Border pedagogy is also important for its value as a counter-narrative to unilateral or dualistic, point/counterpoint perspectives. Border pedagogy allows for participant engagement with multiple cultural codes, experiences, and languages. Through this approach, codified descriptions are critiqued and limitations are challenged.

A central part of becoming as a person and an educator is to better understand oneself, one's teaching, and how students are affected by the ideals being modeled. Border pedagogy requires and understanding of one's personal existence "within social, political, and cultural boundaries that are both multiple and historical in nature and that place particular demands on a recognition and pedagogical appropriation of differences" (Giroux, 1988, p. 176). By contemplating differences, educators deepen understandings of their own personal discourses and employ dialectical approaches to further reflect on their own politics, values, and pedagogy. Personal histories and narratives can then be places within the contexts of domination and resistance. It is equally important for teachers to help students find a language for critically examining the historically and socially constructed forms by which they live (Giroux, 1988).

Border pedagogy links directly with democratic education and seeks to extend the quality of life for all involved with its processes. It provides an acknowledgment of the nature of shifting borders. It also connects schooling and education with current struggles for democratic societies (Giroux, 2005).

Giroux (2005) lists the following theoretical considerations to be contemplated:

1) The category of border signals a recognition of those epistemological, political, cultural, and social margins that structure the language of

history, power, and difference. The category of border also prefigures cultural criticism and pedagogical processes as a form of border crossing.
2) It also speaks to the need to create pedagogical conditions in which students become border crossers in order to understand otherness in its own terms, and to further create borderlands in which diverse cultural resources allow for the fashioning of new identities within existing configurations of power.
3) Border pedagogy makes visible the historically and socially constructed strengths and limitations of those places and borders we inherit and that frame our discourses and social relations. Moreover, as a part of a broader politics of difference (Giroux, 2005, p. 21).

Border Pedagogy in U.S./Mexico Contexts

Numerous studies have noted the particular need for border pedagogy on the U.S. and Mexico border, as well as Latinx students who reside in other parts of the United States. The research on border pedagogy in U.S./Mexico border contexts and has served to build upon Giroux's earlier works, and in many cases, apply theoretical concepts to practical applications in border schools (Bejarano, 2005; Cashman & McDermott, 2013; Cline & Necochea, 2006; Delgado Bernal et al., 2009; Necochea & Cline, 2005; Prieto & Villenas, 2012; Reza-López et al., 2014; Reyes & Garza, 2005; Romo & Chavez, 2006). Moreover, Ramirez et al. (2016) put forth the increase of immigrant and refugee populations throughout U.S. communities has led to border pedagogy studies in non-U.S./Mexico border communities. Rios (2013) uncovered the struggles of students who self-described as Mexicans, Mexican-Americans, and immigrants. Accordingly, high school students identified injustices and expressed their desires for curricula that explores the complexities of borderlands.

These works follow on the writings of Anzaldúa (1987), who argued U.S./Mexico border youth have been that historically marginalized in their education, both inside and outside of schooling. Accordingly, border pedagogy must take on indigenous, non-Western interpretations for "Latino/a youth to understand that their cultural roots and differences are rich and significant to their development as human beings" (Ramirez et al., 2016, p. 303).

Border pedagogy, when put into practice, serves as a means of providing students with better contemplation and clarification of their positions in a region that crosses the international border of two countries (Flores & Clark, 2002). Embedded within the discourses of border pedagogy are the goals of transformative education (Garza, 2007; Giroux, 1991; Romo & Chavez, 2006). Romo and Chavez (2006) documented the way in which teachers engaged youth in border pedagogy. The authors chronicled the manner in which teachers integrated border pedagogy to support student development. Their research also found border pedagogy is important when engaging students in conversations about their culture and identity within border contexts. According to Romo and Chavez (2006):

> Border pedagogy encourages tolerance, ethical sophistication, and openness. In short, border pedagogy works to decolonize and revitalize learning and teaching to promote liberty and justice for all. Border pedagogy particularly engages K-12 students in multiple references that constitute different cultural codes, experiences, and languages to help them construct their own narratives and histories, and revise democracy through sociocultural negotiation. (p. 143)

Cline and Necochea's (2006) documented the significant dispositions needed to enact border pedagogy with youth. The study demonstrated that teachers who were flexible and culturally sensitive, and had a passion for borderland education were more successful in the teaching and learning of border pedagogy.

The goals of border pedagogy coincide with the educational goals of promoting literate, critical, and independent learners (Reyes & Garza, 2005). As educators strive to meet the needs of English language learners on the U.S.-Mexico border, who have distinctive family traditions and cultural identities, their work has implications for social studies education outside of geopolitical border regions. Garza (2007) examined changes in border educators after cultural exchanges that engaged teachers in systemic dialogue and physical visits to schools on both sides of the U.S.-Mexico border. Garza found that conversations among educators on the California-Mexico border area promoted an interconnectedness among educators in the borderlands. Participants in Garza's study learned through a transnational dialogue that they could inform and strengthen each other's educational practices. Educators reconsidered how Mexican influences affected local U.S. schools.

Reyes and Garza (2005) conducted a cross-border study with teachers on both sides of the Tijuana, Mexico, and San Diego, U.S. border. Educators learned from their peers on each side, and, in turn, reflected on their own practices. Reyes and Garza (2005) recommend the design of a flexible, binational curriculum for students. The development of such a curriculum would require those who live far from international borders to share in the work of becoming border crossers, or individuals who are able to traverse ideological boundaries. According to Necochea and Cline (2005), border pedagogy stands in stark contrast to a system that promotes social Darwinism and categorizes students and teachers in a way that exacerbates societal inequities. Left unchecked, schools become complicit with the government in this process of social stratification. Democracy, social justice, and equity should be "integral components of schools in diverse society that purports to provide opportunities for all children, including those in the borderlands" (Necochea & Cline, 2005, p. 131). Necochea and Cline (2008) put forth that successful borderland educators were deemed more sensitive to their students' experience and the identities within their classroom. Border pedagogy, as it turns out, is a highly effective approach to educating important interdisciplinary, transnational issues (Reyes & Garza, 2005). Research has also noted the immense importance of border pedagogy for teacher educators and preservice teachers. Romo and Chavez (2006) studied the most salient characteristics of border pedagogy educators. Their findings indicated preservice teachers needed to recognize and contemplate the complexities of class, nationality, language, culture, and race. In turn, future educators need to reflect on their own personal histories and various contexts of privilege. Salinas et al. (2016) also argue the need for border pedagogy in teacher education. Accordingly, they assert the following:

> The purpose of highlighting border pedagogies in teacher education is to engage candidates in learning about the skills and knowledge that have been historically and culturally developed in spaces that enable individuals, families, and the community to thrive. (p. 324)

Although border pedagogy is not geographically limited to the U.S./México border, the complexities of the U.S. and Mexico border region highlight the need for educating and promoting intellectual border crossings.

Salinas et al. (2016) put forth conditions in which Latinx students must continually cross educational borders. First, Latinx students are seeking full enfranchisement and social justice within the dominant educational system. Second, the intra-group diversity among Latinx student populations should be valued. Accordingly, "panethnicity may draw (Latinx) together for multiple reasons, but their shared histories, experiences, and lives are not without distinct differences that poignantly emphasize a Latinidad" (Salinas et al., 2016, p. 333.) When Latinx students obtain knowledge of their own histories of civil disobedience they begin to question how they have been informed and positioned by official histories. According to Reza-Lopez et al. (2014), border pedagogy does not necessarily provide all students with a path for success in education, but it does question and change the way marginalized Latinx youth are educated.

U.S. and Canada Border Contexts

Easton and Hewson (2018) consider border pedagogy through the lenses of exceptionalism. Much has been written of the concept of U.S. exceptionalism and how it affects the perspectives of U.S. educators. However, this study analyzes Canadian exceptionalism through filters of border pedagogy. The authors note,

> Our experiences teaching the Canada-US border continue to encourage us to imagine strategies that provoke critical, transformative thinking in our students. We wonder, though, if the resiliency of an Anglo-centred Canadian exceptionalism means that simply encouraging students to become border crossers is sufficient to effect the kind of critical awareness they will require to engage with the processes of indigenization underway at our institutions and across Canada. (Easton & Hewson, 2018, pp. 78–79)

They argue for momentous changes in the Canadian education system to counter what they refer to as "the persistent myth of Canadian moral superiority based on racial tolerance, multiculturalism" (Easton & Hewson, 2018, p. 79). The need for an emphasis on treaties as a part of Canadian border pedagogy is noted. Explicitly, their work brings to prominence the importance of treaties with not only the United States on Canada's southern geographic boundaries, but also accords maintained or broken with Canada's indigenous peoples, many of whom live in northern regions of Canada. Hence, Easton and Hewson advance the importance of border pedagogy for discourses on both northern and southern borders of Canada. The authors recommend teaching of the need for enforcement of environmentally friendly treaties with Canada's indigenous populations, regardless of the regions inhabited. Accordingly, they ponder "if an entirely different pedagogy might be required to address the Canada/US border" (Easton & Hewson, 2018, p. 79). Thus, their work broadens perspectives of how and where border pedagogy should be put into practice. Easton and Hewson (2018) sum up their findings by stating,

> A border pedagogy oriented toward treaty pedagogy offers a way to teach the Canada-US border in a way that accounts for the specific historical forces that shaped it. Treaty pedagogy suggests that in respecting the past and the treaties that have structured it, we might learn to live together more respectfully, now and into the future. (p. 80)

Cashman and McDermott (2011) interviewed and observed ten secondary social studies teachers in three secondary schools in two eastern Ontario, Canada, communities. Their main goal was to investigate the perceptions of these Ontario educators toward U.S transnational policies in a country geographically, economically, and culturally linked with the United States. The study produced salient distinctions beyond the aforementioned interrelationships. Important discourses in Canadian classrooms compared health care systems, respective domestic policies, the effects of U.S. gun culture and violence on Canadian culture, the impact of U.S. media and pop culture on Canadian society, separation of church and state, the escalating and polarizing crescendos of political campaigns, multiculturalism, NAFTA, and multinational corporations in both countries. Evident throughout the study was a general theme of Canada as the "mouse" and the United States as the "elephant" on the global stage (Cashman & McDermott, 2011, p. 165). The findings of this study indicated U.S. educators should be provided the opportunity to cross borders and learn from the narratives of Canadian educators.

Border Pedagogy in U.S./Cuba Contexts

Cuba sits only 84 nautical miles from the southernmost point of the U.S. state of Florida, but boundaries between the United States and Cuba can seem impenetrable due to historical and geopolitical tensions. Border pedagogy has been conspicuously absent. Lutjens (2007) argues that we can learn lessons about social theory, critique, and praxis in educational settings by analyzing Cuba's experiences. There is a need for more scholarship on Cuban educational policy and schooling practices. Moreover, the level of interest in Cuban education has dramatically increased. Garii advocates recognizing how educational and political structures impact our perspectives to better contemplate and analyze our engagement in transnational dialogue. According to Garii (2014, p. 17), "We must recognize our inherent biases that color interpretations of our work."

Cashman (2019) examines how teachers in Cuban classrooms engage in discourses on Cuban and U.S. relations, including an examination of how shared historical and territorial issues are taught in Cuba. The research reveals how border pedagogy has been nonexistent in investigations of the content and teaching approaches employed by Cuban educators. There has been negligible analysis of how Cuban educators facilitate discourses U.S. history and policies in Cuban curricula. Therefore, Cashman (2019) recommends that U.S. and Cuban educational communities further engage in transnational exchanges and discourses addressing ongoing issues facing the two educational systems. Recommendations from this research include further allocation of resources for educational efforts on national, state, and local levels so border pedagogy and praxis between Cuban and the United States become reality. Ultimately, the study argues that pragmatic hope offers possibilities for an emergent third space for Cuban and U.S. relations, including educational exchanges (Cashman, 2019).

The importance of considering border pedagogy in U.S. contexts with Mexico, Canada, and Cuba is that unilateralism no longer takes center stage.

Self-interests prevail within and across border settings, but border pedagogy entails a dialogue that uncovers hidden motives and points of contention. In essence, border pedagogy serves as educational approaches that peel away the layers of historical, societal, cultural, economic, and political interests that separate governments and societies, and, moreover, serve as barriers to transnational understandings, cooperation, and collaboration. In times of transborder health crises and social unrest, transnational support and teamwork emerge as even more essential for the promotion of shared communications and problem-solving for health emergencies and conflict resolution within our societies.

How, then, do we characterize border pedagogy in the present, and what should be our objectives for border pedagogy? According to Kasanjian (2011),

> Border pedagogy is continually redefining itself, creating a new vocabulary for expression, and new lenses for understanding. . . . It is a process of interpretation, reinterpretation, and in a constant state of problematizing itself. (p. 378)

With the proliferation of a deadly viral pandemic and continued social protests and upheaval, border pedagogy can serve the purpose of those challenging dominant and oppressive institutions worldwide. Thus, this is a crucial time for the applied knowledge, decision making, informed actions, and policies associated with border pedagogy.

Chapter 3

An Examination of Place-Based Pedagogies

INTRODUCTION

As noted in the previous chapter, research in transnational settings is informed through broader understandings of border pedagogy. Theoretical approaches to place-based education also complement border pedagogy as perceptions of place are central to understandings concepts of borders, spatial interactions, and education across borders. Smith (2002) argues place-based education can be adapted and individualized to fit the characteristics of particular places, and can promote connections among schools and children's lives. Sobel (2005) defines place-based education as the process of using the local community and environment as a starting point to teach essential concepts in both individual subjects across the curriculum. Students engage in hands-on, project-based learning experiences with goals of improving academic achievement and engaging students within their communities. Learning involves development of an appreciation for the natural environment and the importance of contributing to the overall society as an educated citizen.

PLACE-BASED PEDAGOGY

According to Smith (2016), the roots of place-based education date to traditionally informal schooling processes. Place-based education focuses on the incorporation of local knowledge, skills, and issues into the curriculum, and involves an effort to restore learning experiences that were once the basis of children's acculturation and socialization prior to the invention of formal schools. Prior to the invention of formal education, children learned within the context of their families, neighborhoods, and communities. Initiation rites played a role along with informal learning designed to prepare children for their eventual roles and responsibilities as adults. Once established, schools and formal education came to dominate the lives of young people with the passage of compulsory school attendance laws. John Dewey observed schools as they had developed by the 1890s as problematic as what transpired in classrooms was generally unrelated to children's real-world experiences. Teachers felt a loss of curiosity among children in classrooms (Smith, 2016). Dewey attempted to alter this situation by establishing the University of Chicago Lab where he sought to transform the classroom into a small community. Dewey's ideas are often associated with hands-on learning, something that is indeed central to his educational vision (Smith, 2016).

This approach was especially well-received in rural schools. Teachers and administrators in several rural schools throughout the United States implemented curriculum and instructional approaches tied to local culture. Beginning with the *Foxfire* project in Rabun County High School in northern Georgia, teachers invited their students to engage in cultural journalism, investigating traditional practices and history, and subsequently publishing their findings in regional journals or books. Foxfire, named after a term for local bioluminescence caused by fungi on decaying wood, started as a class project at a Rabun County High School in northern Georgia. Foxfire started in 1966, when an English teacher in Rabun County was having a difficult time engaging his students. He allowed students design their owns lessons, and discovered their choices were based on documenting the mountain culture all around them (Shapiro, 2016). Students interviewed neighbors and wrote a series of articles, which were so well-supported and popular, that a quarterly magazine and edited book were produced in 1972. Other books followed, and within 10 years more than 9 million copies of Foxfire were sold. Today, specialized Foxfire books focus on cooking, winemaking, religion, and music (Danovich, 2017).

For over fifty years Foxfire students have recorded the disappearing traditions of Appalachia, and the stories of the region's mountain folks. Students have recounted the stories of community members such as blacksmiths, moonshiners, and woodworkers. Projects modeled after Foxfire have popped up in schools from Maine to the U.S. Southwest and to Alaska in the United States. Ideas from the program have also been applied internationally. Books that grew out of that student-produced magazine became national best-sellers. Of the twenty-one Foxfire books published twenty are still in print. In 1974, the proceeds of the publications were used to create a museum, the Foxfire Museum & Heritage Center in Mountain City, dedicated to preserving Appalachian culture (Shapiro, 2016).

Today, students at Rabun County High School produce two double-issues of *The Foxfire Magazine* each school year. The publications focus on the remarkable stories and extraordinary talents of people in the surrounding communities and beyond, and on living cultural traditions and Appalachian heritage. Additionally, *Foxfire Today*, a digital publication is created by fifth and sixth grade students from Rabun County Elementary and Middle Schools. It follows in the footsteps of *The Foxfire Magazine* and involves project-based learning (Foxfire, 2019).

Many early experiments in place-based education were influenced by Foxfire Program. As part of a statewide organization called Program for Academic Excellence in Rural Schools (PACERS) students throughout rural Alabama were provided with opportunities to learn how to build greenhouses and low-cost housing, start gardens and aquaculture labs, publish community newsletters, and set up their own businesses (Smith, 2016).

In the late 1990s, the Annenberg Rural Challenge funded schools in thirteen sites from Alaska to South Texas participated in a process of connecting children to the communities where they lived to improve local living conditions and create opportunities in their rural surroundings. the local and its possibilities. During the 1990s in Montana, the Montana Heritage Project, a ten-year statewide partnership with the Library of Congress in Washington, D.C., engaged students in the collection and publishing of oral histories and archival research. In this manner, learners made connections among their own personal histories with the historical accounts of other individuals who resided in their own towns and regions (Smith, 2016).

Much of the research on place-based pedagogy reference Gruenewald's 2003 publications, "The Best of Both Worlds: A Critical Pedagogy of Place" and "Foundations of Place: A Multidisciplinary Framework for Place-Conscious Education" as frames of reference. According to Gruenewald (2003b), a "US emphasis on state-mandated standards for teachers and students tends to work toward uniform skills and outcomes limits the inclusion of place in school curricula" (p. 619). Gruenewald (2003a) was influenced by the work of Freire (2005) and developed the theory that a critical pedagogy of place needed to focus on the following:

- Working with students to decolonize accepted notions of how both people and land are oppressed by dominant institutions aimed primarily at privileging the few at the expense of the many; and
- Providing students with the opportunity to restore damaged social and ecological systems, or the process of *reinhabitation.*

According to Gruenewald (2003b), political pressures for higher test scores have narrowed interpretations of achievement. Gruenewald maintains test scores are not truly reflective of enduring learning, and recommends a curriculum more related to the life experiences of students while simultaneously connected with larger, global issues. Students display advanced understandings on trustworthy, reveal-what-has-been-learned assessments after they have engaged in community-centered studies, provided those assessments have been tied to the larger ecosphere. In this manner, students are connected to community life. In "The Best of Both Worlds" (Gruenewald, 2003a) puts forth place-based pedagogy provides a narrative and awareness of local and regional histories, sociocultural, and geopolitical realities. These experiences, in turn, are then linked to global events, policies, and decisions that impact their locales. The realities stand in contrast to educational reform movements that omit considerations of place and fail to question economic development policies as those decisions affect their local communities.

A critical pedagogy of place interrogates the intersection between cultures and ecosystems. A standards-based paradigm of accountability is questioned for its isolation from learning environments outside of schools. Gruenewald (2003a) advocates a reimagining of conventional notions of achievement; definitions of school achievement must begin to take into consideration the quality of community life. Smith (2002) argues that place-based education is particular to locales, thus ensuring most curriculum models unsuited. Smith recommends educational research on local cultural studies, local nature studies, community issue-investigation and problem-solving, local internships and entrepreneurial opportunities, and community decision making. Accordingly, educational research is important for developing communities of learners who protect, conserve, and renovate their environs.

In "Foundations of Place" Gruenewald (2003b) critiques policies implemented under the guises of school reform and high stakes testing when he puts forth the following:

> Contemporary school reform takes little notice of place. The emphasis on state-mandated standards for teachers and students tends to work toward uniform, if sometimes segregated, skills and outcomes that schools are expected to promote. The pressure of "accountability" and the publication of standardized test scores in the news media reinforce the assumption that student, teacher, and school achievement can be measured by classroom routines alone and that the only kind of achievement that really matters is individualistic, quantifiable, and statistically comparable. (p. 619)

Gruenewald argues cultural contexts of education are not considered, nor are problematic ideas of accountability taken into account. Holt (1989) views processes of teaching and learning from community life provide for ongoing, continuous learning by students and teachers alike. Place-conscious education integrates educational discourses and practices beyond the four walls of traditional classrooms. Teachers and students engage with the community and with the political processes of what shapes the local environs.

A critique of place-based learning, as theorized and practiced, is that it has largely focused on environmental studies and has underplayed the role of culture within studies of place. Raffan's (1992) dissertation develops a framework for place-responsive experience from a geographically specific cultural group with strong connections to "land as teacher," connections that include the dependence on land for food and survival. In fact, studies of place and education should broaden meanings of place as a part of educational inquiry. Raffan critiques investigations into the philosophical constructs of place and sense of place that are not grounded in the lived experience of a specific cultural group. Raffan's (1992) work focuses on sensory perception and bioregional learning, storytelling, and other varied insights. Critical geographers, in turn, ground their analyses in social rather than ecological space and consider human interactions with individuals and groups over interactions with the land. In *A Pedagogy of Place*, Wattchow and Brown (2011) attempt bridging land and water with socially critical perspectives toward place. Wattchow and Brown (2011) suggest future directions for the movement of place-conscious and place-responsive education, a movement that should continue to promote multiple and contested definitions of place.

Demarest (2014) put forth place-based education provides educators with the ability to structure curriculum around authentic investigations to engage students within the community. In the pursuit of local questions, teachers and students develop partnerships with specific locales, community organizations, commercial enterprises, and individuals that provide the context for content acquisition, engaged learning, and meaningful community service. Using local questions as the foundation of curriculum design integrates elements of a number of different educational traditions, including inquiry, standards-based curriculum design, project- and problem-based learning, and associated best practices. Accordingly, place-based education complements additional pedagogical approaches.

Several examples and models of place-based education have been put in place outside the United States. There is evidence of place-based educational programs in Canada, the United Kingdom, Norway, Australia, India, Bhutan, New Zealand, Japan, El Salvador, and China. Educators representative of seemingly disparate cultural contexts have been drawn to teaching and learning approaches that involve getting students out of the classroom and into their communities. Whether these teachers, administrators, and schools refer to their approaches as place-based pedagogy or not, the approaches employed are being put in practice to better involve their students in purposeful personal and community engagement.

Chapter 3

ALASKA PLACE-BASED EDUCATION

Among the many places where the Foxfire Program inspired local initiatives was the state of Alaska. The Alaska Rural Systemic Initiative (AKRSI) observed schools were unable to integrate into the social fabric of many rural communities as an indication of the critical requisite for new systemic approach to educational conditions in rural Alaska. AKRSI was created with the goals of implementing educational renewal of structures, content, and processes to better engage Alaska Native people in the application of Native and non-Native scientific knowledge. AKRSI also sought to uncover the untapped potential of indigenous knowledge systems as a foundation for rural/Native education (Emekauwa, 2004). Place-based education was officially promoted for Alaskan rural education. Support was received from the National Science Foundation and the Annenberg Rural Challenge. AKRSI sought to document indigenous ways of knowing, develop pedagogical practices, and design new curricula. The ongoing efforts of AKRSI were to be integrated with Western knowledge systems (Emekauwa, 2004).

What motivated the rationale for AKRSI were findings of the failures of efforts to Westernize Native Alaskans. There was no recognition of the strength and resiliency of thousand-year-old indigenous knowledge systems. Accordingly, credit was not given for a deep understanding of and respect for the natural world and the natural order of life. Unwritten, collective, generational wisdom was passed on through stories, observation, and practice. It was a system that enabled Native peoples to flourish in a land where survival depended on intimate knowledge of and harmony with the environment (Emekauwa, 2004). AKRSI sought to couple indigenous knowledge systems with Western science to form the foundation for a new, place-based, culturally responsive, and academically rigorous education that met the needs of Native children.

Emekauwa (2004) noted that building by using AKRSI's approaches an educational system with a strong foundation in the local culture began producing effects in all indicators of school success, including dropout rates, college attendance, and standardized achievement test scores. AKRSI's place-based focus has reached far beyond the twenty rural school districts with which it has worked most directly. Sharing Our Pathways (2000) documented findings of other accomplishments including: (a) increased interest in teacher education and college enrollment among Native students; (b) a change to more authentic assessment and evaluation practices, including valuing indigenous knowledge and cultural imperatives; (c) state-adopted standards for culturally responsive schools, including cultural standards for students, educators, schools, elders, community, and curriculum; (d) guidelines for nurturing culturally healthy youth, reinforcing indigenous languages, promoting culturally responsive school boards; and for preparing culturally responsive teachers; (e) effective revisions teacher preparation to include teaching methodologies that incorporate indigenous ways, values, and culture; and (f) the development of a section of the Alaska Curriculum Frameworks entitled *Native Ways of Knowing*. Moreover, Emekauwa (2004) adds what developed was a recognition of the educational potential and validity of the indigenous knowledge systems still in use in many rural villages throughout Alaska.

U.S. SOUTHWEST PLACE-BASED EDUCATION

Another example of a study influenced by the Foxfire Program was local history projects conducted in a Southwestern U.S. high school classroom located in Central New Mexico community (Cashman, 2005). Research was conducted in a community that had been established in 1740, yet students rarely discussed the importance of landmarks and historical treasures that, in some cases, were in their own backyards. Many students were aware of the fact that their ancestors had resided in the area since the early eighteenth century; on the other hand, a significant number of students had recently moved to New Mexico. Community pride was very much in evidence; however, high school students were not always as engrossed as their parents with regard to the community's noteworthy characteristics. Some students felt that their local community lacked distinguishing features; local attributes appeared to be taken for granted. Few students felt that they possessed enlightening personal histories, and even less students considered publicly sharing knowledge of their own local cultures until they were assigned a local history project in their American history classes. Students were soon engaged in approaches that paralleled the strategies of the Foxfire Program (Starnes et al., 1999; Wigginton, 1991). My goal was to personally engage my students with the past and present processes of history. Wigginton (1991) notes students of a culture may not have more than superficial notions of their own cultures. Independent student research and inquiry, where aspects of culture are discovered and brought to a level of consciousness and examined, is requisite. Students are better able to move into the larger world to become responsible citizens when they appreciate their own culture and acknowledge its contributions (Wigginton, 1991). Students needed to conduct background research, identify and interview experts and other informants, and present their information to their classmates. According to Starnes et al. (1999), the following are the necessary components of student-centered projects: learner choice, design, and revision; the teacher's roles of facilitator and collaborator; academic integrity; active learning;

peer teaching; small group work and teamwork; connections between the classroom work, the surrounding communities, and the world beyond the community; an audience beyond the teacher for learner work; new activities modified from old activities; creativity; reflection; and rigorous, ongoing assessment and evaluation.

The findings of this study indicated students appreciated history when they could contribute to the subject with their own personal historical accounts. Students drew upon a vast collection of experiences that included both recent history and centuries of community annals. An abundance of diverse historical accounts were waiting to be uncovered, recollected, and/or retold.

AN EXAMPLE OF PLACE-BASED EDUCATION IN CHINA

Lam (2016) cited the Foxfire Program as a key influence for research conducted in a village of about 500 people in central China. At dusk, villagers gather and sit on wooden benches behind the projector. Students from the village elementary school's fifth grade class investigated and collected oral histories on the topic of local water issues and history, including the importance of water sources and changes to local water sources and supplies over time. Students had visited local rivers to "observe and record the mechanisms through which water is diverted for industrial usage as well as sources of pollution that are affecting the rivers" (Lam, 2016, p. 4). Students went on to share their findings with their elders in a community presentation. According to Lam,

> Some villagers in the audience contributed information or personal stories reflected in the presentation, but still, they leave with new insights. Some learn for the first time how exactly water is brought to the taps in their courtyards, others learn about the different perspectives and water use of people from different generations or from other villages at different points along the local rivers, while still others gain a greater awareness of threats to local water sources and the importance of conservation. (2016, p. 4)

Teachers and students learned about the Foxfire Program and discovered they shared many of the goals and principles of the Foxfire approaches. Lam (2016) found there are educators in China who, although working in vastly different contexts, share a commitment to democratic education in which students have a significant voice in making decisions about the goals and process of their learning. There are educators both in the United States and in China who share common ideals of democratic education, who are

COMMON THREADS IN VARIOUS COUNTRIES

Educators in the United States and international settings report the initial planning for place-based education took extra efforts. With that noted, they reported more rigorous, varied, and in-depth learning products completed and submitted by their students (Demarest, 2014). Moreover, by engaging their students in place-based projects local investigations were designed to be more self-directed, inquiry-based, experiential. Demarest (2014) notes,

> The ability to facilitate investigations implies a skilled ability to structure learning around questions and to claim time for students to explore, experiment, and interpret. In inquiry based learning, the teacher is a coach, problem-poser, and facilitator. (p. 5)

Educators also address curriculum standards, while remaining responsive to the individual needs of students. In effect, educators take on the challenges of remaining true to the existing curriculum incorporating place-based curricula that include forms of assessment that require personal investigations with the people, places, and things outside of the traditional classroom. Teachers also create opportunities for the development of writing skills and knowledge of local history, as well as a vision of personal goals including community service, professional opportunities, and employment (Demarest, 2014). In this manner, educators facilitate understanding of the local environment as it relates to larger national and global circumstances. Greenwood (2013) states "Places teach us and shape our identities and relationships" (p. 93). Demarest (2014) puts forth global understanding is built from local learning. In other words "Local places provide the specific contexts from which reliable knowledge of global relationships emerge" (Demarest, 2014, p. 13). Elder (1999) points out that knowing a place well should not exclude the ability to understand others. Educators "should cultivate a perspective of attentiveness to place—wherever one is—that lets one be in a new place too, with a strong sense of appreciation and responsibility for it" (Elder, 1999, p. 28). Educators in the Alaskan Native Knowledge Network support the "efficacy of an educational system that is grounded in the deep knowledge associated with a particular place, upon which a broader knowledge of the world can be built" (Barnhardt, 2008, p. 132).

Smith and Sobel (2010) merge the terms place- and community-based to underline the highly civic nature of this learning as students build authentic partnerships with community members. Demarest (2014) recommends that students investigate local issues in their communities to better form a foundation for contemplating their personal roles and responsibilities. From these starting points students may build on their reflections to better consider and envision their roles as part of a more global citizenry. Contrary to what might be argued, local understandings should not promote provincialism and diminish the importance and opportunities for global understandings.

An important part of place-based education is the promotion of learning about and within our inhabited and uninhabited spaces. Thus both ecological footprints and the way we interact with one another as well as the environment are key components of place-based education. Greenwood (2013) writes: "A theory of place that is concerned with the quality of human-world relationships first acknowledges that places themselves have something to say. Human beings, in other words, must learn to listen" (p. 98).

Gruenewald (2003), puts forth, "By promoting a pedagogy for student engagement in community life, place-based educators embrace aims beyond preparing students for market competition. This generalization about place-based education signal both similarity to and difference from critical pedagogy" (p. 7). The idea here is not that educators should avoid the realities of these human-created crises, but that we should pursue pedagogical strategies that honor a learners' developmental readiness for engaging with complex ecological themes. Bowers (2008) maintains there should be no assumption that critical theorists have solutions for how other cultures should self-determine place-based education.

On the other hand, a critical pedagogy of place aims to contribute to the production of educational discourses and practices that explicitly examines the place-specific nexus among environment, culture, and education. It is a pedagogy linked to cultural and ecological politics and other socio-ecological traditions that interrogate the intersection between cultures and ecosystems.

THE FUTURE OF PLACE-BASED EDUCATION

The growing national interest in project-based learning should be coupled with the recognition that situating local issue projects in students' home communities deepens the meaning and impacts of learning. Current trends and movement away from standardized education signal interest in place-based education, and the possibilities for future realization and implementation of place-based pedagogies. Place-based education has been found to produce vital links among students with their home communities and regions, while, at the same time, students develop problem-solving and collaboration skills. Students also acquire a sense of responsibility for the natural environment and its inhabitants. Among them is instilled an awareness of personal capacities to be change agents. Thus, place-based education can be an effective way of promoting student engagement and active participation in their own personal development and education (Smith, 2016).

Transborder research furthers overall comparative knowledge on a sense of place, including historical, economic, societal, and environmental issues. According to Smith (2016), social and environmental challenges, in particular, require individuals to possess knowledge and experiences associated with place-based education. Moreover, if more sustainable and just societies are to be promoted, then activism and enlightened views of the local, national, and global will be required. Given recent developments worldwide, such as the COVID-19 pandemic, Black Lives Matters movement, and social upheaval as a response to institutionalized racism, violence, and White supremacy, place-based education serves as a necessary starting point for contemplating the interconnectedness of local issues with wider national and international questions of belonging, social justice, equity, environmental destruction, climate change, and social meliorism.

Chapter 4

Transborder Dialogue

Intersections of Meliorism, Heteroglossia, Nepantla, and Dialogic Feminism

INTRODUCTION

This chapter will examine how effective transborder dialogue intersects with the concepts and theoretical constructs related to meliorism, heteroglossia, nepantla, and dialogic feminism. According to William James (1906), meliorism exists halfway between optimism and pessimism, and treats the salvation of the world as a probability rather than a certainty or impossibility. Bakhtin (1981) describes heteroglossia as a *reflection* in language of varying ways to evaluate, conceptualize, and experience the world. It is the convergence in language or speech of personal perspectives on the world, descriptions of the world in words, and epistemology. Nepantla is a term from the Nahuatl-speaking people in sixteenth-century Mexico. In Gloria Anzaldúa's (2002) view, this period of Spanish colonization was a time where individuals experienced a loss of control and suffered anxiety and confusion as a result. Mignolo (2000) describes nepantla as a feeling of being "in between," a position placed on the indigenous people of Mexico by the Spanish colonizers. Dialogic feminism is described by Puigvert (2012) as the inclusion of diverse women's voices in dialogue regarding issues that are of concern to all of them. This has involved the creation of new spaces for interaction and dialogue between academic women, including female professors and researchers, and women who belong to vulnerable groups, such as non-academic women, immigrant women, or women from ethnic minorities.

Chapter 4

MELIORISM

Meliorism should be at the core of all educational efforts. True educators have chosen their professions to provide constructive learning environments, rather than simply play the roles of knowledge keepers focused on promoting themselves. According to Koopman (2006),

> Meliorism, holding together pluralism with humanism, is the thesis that we are capable of creating better worlds and selves. Pluralism says that better futures are possible, humanism that possibilities are often enough decided by human energies, and meliorism that better futures are made real by our effort. Meliorism, then, is best seen as humanism and pluralism combined and in confident mood. Melioristic confidence offers a genuine alternative to both pessimism and optimism. These two moods, almost universally proffered by modern philosophers, share a common assumption that progress or decline is inevitable. Meliorism, on the other hand, focuses on what we can do to hasten our progress and mitigate our decline. (p. 107)

Meliorism is also at the heart of democratic principles and democratic classrooms. Meliorism is also at the core of pragmatism. Koopman (2006) views "pragmatism as developing the philosophical consequences of meliorism, while understanding democracy as developing its political and ethical consequences" (p. 107).

Melioristic efforts seek to better a system in the home context, with ideas, approaches, and policies that are influenced by educational systems outside of one's national context (Wilson, 2003). Social meliorists believe that education is a tool to reform society and create change for the better. This socialization goal is based on the power of the individual's intelligence and the ability to improve on intelligence through education (Kliebard, 2004).

Koopman (2006), well before the current political tensions facing the United States put forth, "We stand in need, today, of hope, most especially the strong and flexible form of hope we find in pragmatism. It is hope that credits the confidence necessary for melioration" (Koopman, 2006, p. 112). Koopman also puts forth pragmatism has been associated with American democracy but cautions it "should not be mistaken for self-congratulatory nationalism" (2006, p. 113). Accordingly, pragmatic meliorism encourages renewal and possibilities for a manifestation of "better values in the world" (Koopman, 2016, p. 113).

Although meliorism is based on confidence, effort is integral to meliorism, and efforts must be exerted (James, 1906). Meliorism is based on action that is influenced by various types of hope, including habits of hope (Shade, 2001). If heteroglossia serves as the basis for dialogic principles, then social meliorism is key to the contemplation of why critical border praxis is a requisite in an age of never-ending wars and conflict. Social meliorism combines pluralism with humanism and serves as the thesis that we are capable of creating better worlds and selves. Moreover, social meliorists believe education is a tool to restructure society and promote social change (Cashman. 2016).

HETEROGLOSSIA

In order to challenge basic assumptions regarding dialogue and dialogic processes, heteroglossic principles undergird efforts to reconsider words, utterances, non-verbal communications, and thoughts. In that manner, dominant discourses can be confronted and reconsidered, if necessary. Bakhtin (1981) refers to discourses that challenge and counter authoritative discourse as *heteroglossia*. An authoritative discourse promotes a single perspective and is described as being unified. It lacks varied voices and perspectives. Heteroglossia, conversely, is a profusion of voices that represent a multitude of viewpoints and perspectives. Moreover, it stands in contrast with an ideology that tries to unify and normalize. Clark and Holquist (1986) maintain heteroglossia, as described by Bakhtin, intersects different language groups, cultures, and classes. Bakhtin put forth heteroglossia guarantees linguistic and intellectual transformation and guards against the promotion of a "single language of truth" or "official language" in a given society, against ossification and stagnation in thought (Clark & Holquist, 1986, p. 22). Heteroglossia includes a multiplicity of discourses, inclusive of those languages that challenge other communications. It also engages us in languages that must be corrected, languages that have been ignored, and languages that have been deemed invisible.

Bakhtin (1981) juxtaposes a unitary language with heteroglossia, as unitary language "gives expression to forces working toward concrete verbal and ideological unification and centralization, which develop in vital connection with the processes of sociopolitical and cultural centralization" (Bakhtin, 1981, p. 271). Bakhtin recommends polyphony in educational settings and describes polyphony as a discursive place. Discourses provide for the conceptualization and carrying out of a polyphonic classroom (DePalma, 2010). In this manner, multiple voices are invited to engage in dialogue and dialogic understandings of truth. A polyphonic classroom promotes dialogic understandings of truth and serves to counter monologic spaces. Moreover, polyphony does not have any specific final form and is always a work in progress (DePalma, 2010). Monologic spaces are occupied by authoritative discourses. According to Bakhtin (1981), an authoritative discourse "demands that we acknowledge it, that we make it our own; it binds us, quite independent of any power it might have to persuade us internally; we encounter it with its authority already fused to it" (p. 342).

Abraham (2014) links this statement to patriarchy, heteronormativity, monolingualism, and Whiteness. An authoritative discourse can be recognized by its need for perfection, accuracy, and inflexibility, and "it remains sharply demarcated, compact and inert; it deems, so to speak, not only quotation marks but a demarcation even more magisterial, a special script, for instance" (Bakhtin, 1981, p. 343). Bakhtin describes authoritative discourses and being static with singular, as opposed to variable, meanings. This discourse is not easy to question because of the historical contexts associated with authority, past and present. To the contrary, "heteroglossic voices will pull against this centralization of thought and normalized ideology and only one way to mean" (Abraham, 2014, p. 11).

Halasek (1992) notes that dialogue corresponds with heteroglossia. Accordingly, dialogue and heteroglossia are both responses to social and cultural breakdowns and criticisms of dominant ideology, hierarchical conditions, and ethnocentrism. Heteroglossia involves multi-voiced discourses, whereas dialogism describes how narrative voices interact. For further comparison, heteroglossia is the hegemony of languages as a disparate condition, and dialogism is the coordination of how these various languages interact. Dialogism is a requisite practice between competing, conflicting, contrary, or contradictory forms of communication. Both heteroglossia and dialogism counter authoritative discourses. Bakhtin (1981) describes authoritative discourse as internally persuasive and dominant. Moreover, the authoritative word is connected to hierarchical powers located and positioned in the past. Authoritative discourses often address political, ethical, moral, or religious issues (Bakhtin, 1981). Authoritative discourses solicit unconditional allegiance and, at times, receive reverence from adherents. According to Bakhtin (1981), the influence of authoritative discourses is a product of traditional perspectives and unquestioned mandates. Moreover, the resulting texts are reflective of the education, history, cultures, and societies that produced the narratives. Bakhtin (1981) also depicts authoritative discourses as powerful and designed to maintain the status quo. Authoritative discourses are often unquestioned and perceived by adherents as nonnegotiable.

Bakhtin (1981) argued that communication reflects other utterances and that words never exist in neutral and impersonal form, but rather as communication that serves others' intentions and are adopted as one's own. Words are appropriated for our own use with varying degrees struggle and with complex heteroglossic effects (DePalma, 2010). Thus, a Bakhtinian dialogic framework promotes an engaging and productive classroom environment through the following:

1. encouraging students to show respect for each other's views even though students are less asked to interrogate assumptions or their own implication in systemic inequities,
2. dialogic engagement that requires a reflection on personal subjectivities to provide contexts and understandings of positions potentially set aside as political, ideological, or religious stances,
3. promotion of a non-threatening learning community that holds promise for emergent spaces after allowances for reflections on personal histories, work experiences, social practices and youth subcultures, ideas developed in other educational offerings, and professional concerns, and
4. engaging with disparate views on how to approach the complexity of any given issue, discovering common ground with peers and educators who possess seemingly contrasting perspectives, and learning how to reach consensus (DePalma, 2010).

Bakhtin (1981) also stressed the need to recognize and challenge internally persuasive discourses within ourselves. Individuals consume elements of authoritative discourses and heteroglossia. Abraham (2014) notes that when these discourses become embedded in a person's way of thinking, then that discourse has become what the internally persuasive discourse. In this case authoritative discourses determine the very bases of our ideological interrelations with the world, the very basis of our behavior, an internally persuasive discourse (Bakhtin, 1981).

NEPANTLA

Nepantla is derived from the Nahuatl word translated as "a place in the middle" or "the middle." It is a term that connotates with Chicano and Latinx anthropology, social commentary, criticism, literature, and art. Nepantla represents a concept of "in-between-ness." The term was employed by Nahuatl-speaking people in Mexico during the sixteenth century. During this time, they were being colonized by Spaniards and the concept of being "in between" was useful to describe how the experience felt (Mignolo, 2000). According to Anzaldúa, nepantla is characterized as a "liminal" space, where multiple forms of reality are viewed simultaneously. This concept is especially relevant to situations where diverse populations have difficulty arriving at any sort of consensus. Promoting understandings of seemingly competing concepts is part of the process of nepantla. Therefore, a noteworthy possible outcome within conditions of nepantla is the development of new and original concepts as a byproduct of current struggles.

The liminal spaces constituting nepantla merit deliberation for all cultures colonized, politically dominated, and subjugated. These particular third spaces developed as a consequence of Spanish conquest of the indigenous inhabitants of what is now Mexico. Religious and cultural institutions were destroyed by a Spanish colonial system that enslaved, decimated, and devastated populations. Fully half of the indigenous inhabitants died from a smallpox plague that was introduced by Spanish colonizers (Román-Odio, 2013). Survivors were forced to labor in the abhorrent conditions of agriculture, construction, and mines of the time period. Indigenous clothing, ornamentation, food, rituals, cultural traditions, and spirituality were considered diabolic and forbidden by law. Natives were coerced to abandon belief systems that paid homage to deities as part of a belief system that provided structure to their lifestyles, including "harvesting, family organization, political, social, and religious structures" (Román-Odio, 2013, p. 52). This social upheaval and shattering of societal and familial connections provided the historical contexts of nepantla.

Nahuatl-speaking people used the concept of nepantla, or the land in the middle, to fathom and endure the imposed conditions of the Spanish conquest. Anzaldúa (1987) applies nepantla to subjects of the U.S. and Mexico borderlands where the dominant culture makes obligatory its economic, political, cultural, and spiritual norms. Anzaldúa employs nepantla as a way of thinking recognizes these internal and external conflicts as serves as "a strategy of crossing that offers the decentered border subject an alternative way to approach colonial ideology" (Román-Odio, 2013, p. 52).

Mignolo (2000) argues nepantla is a condition that allows indigenous descendants to make sense of conflict with Spanish conquistadors, invaders, and missionaries. Accordingly, the Nahua forged nepantla during a time of colonization. Maffie (2007), on the contrary, argues Nahua philosophies and lifestyles of nepantla predated the arrival of Spanish colonizers. Maffie's maintains that nepantla was Nahua societal perspectives long before Spanish invasions of their homelands. Rather, Maffie (2007) puts forth that nepantla is a permanent, as opposed to more recent and temporal, state of liminality within Nahua worldviews.

Thus, Abraham (2014) and Maffie (2007) maintain that nepantla is embedded in the Nahua belief system that places "people and things within a borderland" or within "a dynamic zone of mutual transaction, confluence, unstable and diffuse identity, and transformation" (Maffie, 2007, p. 16). This means that the Nahua held a worldview that sees disorder as a norm for their world. Their concept of nepantla, therefore, serves as perceptions of the human condition and existentialism that run counter to Western philosophies of human-centered environments, absolutism, and rigid dualisms and dichotomies (Anzaldúa, 1987; Bakhtin, 1975/1981; Maffie, 2007).

Anzaldúa (1987) developed the concept of nepantla using a scholarly and literacy structure called, autohistoria/teoria, which is a way to write and create social theory using autobiography embedded in historical events. This, autohistoria/teoría is integral to the advancement of nepantlan pedagogy. Educators must be situated within nepantla themselves "to help situate others in the same state" (Abraham, 2014, p. 3).

Abraham (2014) argues that nepantla is the site of transformation. Accordingly, nepantla is a third space place where one struggles to find equilibrium between cultures and developing perspectives from a culture that was historically oppressed, yet coexisting with the dominant culture (Abraham, 2014). Lizárraga and Gutiérrez (2018) put forth nepantla pedagogies promote "new forms of educational dignity" (p. 39).

Abraham (2014) maintains that through a nepantla pedagogy discourses can be deconstructed and subsequently reconstructed so that educators and their students better view the world through various perspectives previously hidden because of authoritarian discourses. According to Abraham (2014), "Anzaldúa's nepantla is a critique of our society, a society that situates knowledge as absolute, perfect, completely mapped, and unquestionable" (p. 2). Prieto and Villenas (2012) used nepantla to frame their testimonios of their Chicana experience in the United States and in the U.S. educational system. Accordingly, Prieto and Villenas investigated how pedagogy can address cultural and cognitive dissonance, promote social consciousness, and cultures of caring. In this manner, the third space of nepantla entails being in a state of ideological transition (Abraham, 2014). In contrast to Western paradigms that promote stability and seek to repress oppositional ideas and forces, nepantla allows for adaptation, heterogeneity, and dissent (Maffie, 2007; Anzaldúa, 2002).

Anzaldúa (2002) argued that "nepantla is the zone between changes where you struggle to find equilibrium between the outer expression of change and your inner relationship to it" (p. 548–549). Through nepantla, a person sees into other world views and unpacks the myths and histories that are carried with its subjective positionings. Likewise, Maffie (2007) spoke of nepantla as being a process that is "dialectical, transitional, and oscillating; centering as well as destabilizing; and abundant with mutuality and reciprocity" (p. 11). Nepantla is simultaneously destructive and creative," it is also "transformative" (p. 11). Maffie's descriptors of nepantla converge with Anzaldúa's (2002) latest definition of nepantla as the place where you are "seeing through human acts both individual and collective allows you to examine the ways you construct knowledge, identity, and reality, and explore how some of your/others' constructions that violate other people's ways of knowing" (p. 548). These ideas of constructing and deconstructing knowledge from individual and collective acts, seeing our knowledge as violating "other people's ways of knowing" allows me to shift to Bakhtin's concept of ideological becoming and define his terms that encompass how people become who they are through the discourses they consume and produce. Anzaldúa's nepantla is an internally persuasive discourse that provides hope and possibilities for teaching and learning. The influences of internally persuasive discourses are tangible and authentic. Therefore, nepantla, as an internally persuasive discourse, serves as way to disrupt authoritative discourses and to restore balance in a knowledge system.

Nepantla exists as a third space and zone for ideological becoming (Abraham, 2014). According to Anzaldúa (1987) the nepantlan act is an example of ideological becoming. Bakhtin (1981, p. 346) describes ideological becoming as "an intense struggle within us for hegemony" (Bakhtin, 1981, p. 346). Abraham (2014) draws connections between Bakhtin's descriptions of ideological outcomes as "open, in each of the next contexts that dialogize it, this discourse is able to reveal ever newer ways to mean" (Bakhtin, 1981, p. 346). This compares with Anzaldúa (1987) and her accounts of nepantla, where nepantla allows for new "ways to mean" by intentionally and literally writing "a new story to explain the world" (p. 103). When we consider nepantla and ideological becoming as theoretical constructs, room is created for historical and current discourses to be contested, challenged, and transformed (Abraham, 2014). Thus, the conflict between multiple constructions of the world creates pathways to change, analyze, and apply a multiplicity of ideas.

Abraham (2014) suggests that a nepantla pedagogy will, at times, contradict standards and/or challenge lesson objectives. In this pedagogy, there are no standardized approaches and at the forefront is a questioning of conventional knowledge. In this manner, nepantla pedagogy promotes new ways of imagining, conceptualizing, and putting into practice the reconstruction of teaching and learning. The implications for non-dominant group, Latinx student populations in the United States are noteworthy. With regards to Latinx education, Mora (2008) poses the following questions:

1) To what extent do we question and resist organizational and institutional practices that ignore the Latinx community and its needs?
2) To what extent do we struggle against inequities by effectively articulating needed change and by transforming our professions through coalition building (p. 17)?

An examination of concepts associated with nepantla provides possible responses the these questions. Several studies (Necochea & Cline, 2005; Prieto & Villenas, 2012) have incorporated Anzaldúa's notion of nepantla to analyze the rich narratives of Latinx youth in various contexts. Nepantla can be considered as a way to examine the way teachers and students discuss their "cultural identities and *conocimientos* (understandings) to shed light on new ways in which Latino/a students are re-engaging in schools and communities" (Ramirez et al., 2016, p. 304).

Nepantla emerges from concerted self-reflection and naming of marginalization; a creation of a self-authored testimonio that embraces the fluidity of identity (Prieto & Villenas, 2012; Lizárraga & Gutiérrez, 2018). In this manner, students find they learn, reflect, become aware of their own personal histories, and organize their discoveries "for new possible futures in small interactions, through the use of language and gesture" (Lizárraga & Gutiérrez, 2018, p. 42). Students reconceptualize thoughts of themselves. Accordingly, nepantla pedagogies work toward cultivating social justice in classrooms (Delgado et al., 2012; Prieto & Villenas, 2012) and bring attention to the contradictions that emerge in the daily lives of students and youth who are part of a non-dominant culture. Students are then better prepared to take "action for overcoming said contradictions" (Lizárraga & Gutiérrez, 2018, p. 42).

Delgado Bernal et al. (2012) note that "*testimonio* writing has a long and varied history; it is most often seen as a voice from the margins or from the subaltern—a political approach that elicits solidarity from the reader" (p. 364). Testimonios are central to understanding the experiences and struggles of persecuted peoples, or what Grande (2015) has termed survivances. Testimonio approaches attempt to

> incorporate political, social, historical, and cultural histories that accompany one's life experiences as a means to bring about change through consciousness-raising. In bridging individuals with collective histories of oppression, a story of marginalization is re-centered to elicit social change. (Delgado Bernal et al., 2012, p. 342)

Testimonio differs from oral history or autobiography in that it involves the participant in a critical reflection of their personal experience within sociopolitical realities. As such, *testimonio* is pragmatic in that it engages the reader to understand and establish a sense of solidarity as a first step toward social change.

Nepantla is also associated with Grande's (2015) concept of red pedagogy which maintains that indigenous peoples have always been peoples of resistance. Their cultures have stood in "defiance of the vapid emptiness of the bourgeois life" (Grande, 2015, p. 32). This is the spirit that guides the ensuing engagement between critical theory and American Indian education. The hope is for a red pedagogy that not only helps sustain the lifeways of indigenous peoples but also provides an explanatory framework that helps us understand the complex and intersecting vectors of power shaping the historical-material conditions of schools and communities. A logical place to begin this journey of understanding is at the point of the "encounter" examining the various dimensions of conflict and contradiction between the sovereign peoples of the Americas and the colonizers. Grande (2015) asks the question, "Can democracy be built upon the bloody soils of genocide?" (p. 32).

Nepantla serves as a theoretical stance that informs us of the possibilities for efficacious third spaces in education. It negates dualistic approaches and allows for heteroglossia as well as pragmatic hope. It is within this third space that students, including our rapidly growing Latinx student populations, can have their voices heard and respected. Mora (2008) put forth the significance of addressing the critical needs of Latinx students by stating the following:

> I bring more questions than answers, but the questions too often ignored—about our economic, linguistic, and color hierarchies, about the power of naming this country, about dominance and colonization, about unquestioned norms, about the need to create space for ourselves, individually and collectively. (p. 8)

DIALOGIC FEMINISM

Theoretical constructs of nepantla have also informed feminist theory, including dialogic feminism. Feminist theory was originally developed by different groups of academic White women. According to Puigvert (2012), feminists have been crucial in generating societal change and one of the most important movements of the past century, but in many cases positions have "often been representative of the priorities and needs of a very concrete group of women in society, those with higher education and enjoying cultural and socio-economic privileges" (p. 89). During this time of struggle, the concerns of many women, such as those without academic background and from the working class, lacked representation. Puigvert (2012) recommends a dialogic turn of societies and social sciences so more open, diverse models of feminism continue to develop. Of these models, dialogic feminism (Beck-Gernsheim et al., 2003) is designed to engage very diverse women in dialogue so that previously neglected issues of concern can be addressed. Dialogic feminism includes female professors and researchers as well as non-academic women, immigrant women, and women from ethnic minorities in discourses. In this manner, there has been a need for the creation of new spaces for interaction and dialogue.as a part of feminist struggles. The dialogic turn allows for contributions of women who had been excluded from feminist debates historically (De Botton et al., 2005). Contexts where dialogue is taking place, within social movements and under widely varying societal conditions, necessitate the creation of opportunities for all voices being heard so that social contexts can be analyzed and redefined. Dialogic interactions promote greater understandings of the validity of claims and permit situations of "overcoming inequalities and transforming violent power structures" (Puigvert, 2012, p. 92). Halasek (1992) supports Bakhtin's conclusion that all knowledge is created dialogically.

Gore's (1993) critiques both in critical pedagogy and in feminist pedagogy by noting there have been two divergent streams of analysis, each producing silencing and regulating effects. Gore's book is an essential one, and the distinctions uncovered are thought-provoking poststructuralist perspectives on pedagogy. Perhaps Gore should point out the difficulties in avoiding many pedagogical shortcomings. Whereas Gore's own work is highly reflexive and articulates its own positioning, concerns remain of how pedagogy based on the arguments explicated connect with educational practitioners and individuals outside of academia.

Lather (2001) and hooks (2014) argue that the original proponents of critical pedagogy "ignore the feminist, anti-racist, and postcolonial educational projects that overlap with critical pedagogy, and discount the work of Women's Studies and Ethnic Studies programs" (Brueing, 2011, p. 16). According to Brueing (2011), tracing the historical roots of critical theory back to the Frankfurt School only serves to maintain a patriarchal mentality within critical pedagogy, and ignores the need for reconceptualization (hooks, 2003). Grande (2015), moreover, asserts there is an overemphasis on class-based agendas that fail to engage race relations only leads to further marginalization of the political potential for praxis. Gore (1993) and Lather (1998, 2001) assert that a contemporary conceptualization of critical pedagogical praxis should attend to issues related not only to class but also to some of the broader social issues that have historically been less acknowledged, including race, gender, and sexuality.

In Lather's (2001) view, the overlapping "projects" of feminist pedagogies, anti-racist education, and poststructuralism and their intersections with critical pedagogy will only strengthen the justice-oriented purpose of these pedagogies. Lather (2001) puts forth that critical pedagogy is not problematic simply due to the dominance of male authors in the field but rather because of the need for a greater multiplicity of voices and perspectives (Brueing, 2011).

Puigvert (2012) argues there is a need for dialogue that deconstructs and reconstructs our existing understandings. Barriers to effective dialogue endure in various forms. Puigvert (2012), in turn, maintains the current women's movement should address its own shortcomings to contest the inequalities of neoliberal globalization that conflict with the ideals of human rights. In this manner, there is a call for counter-hegemonic praxis and working to achieve women's human rights that challenge and repudiate dominant conceptions. Puigvert (2012) maintains we must create new paths walked by women free of gender violence in all its forms. The following is put forth:

> Among them we find the systemic walls, which are produced by the system itself, such as the bureaucracy of political parties or the strategic actions of the mass media, which block the use of dialogue as a procedure for diverse social actors to reach agreement. (Puigvert, 2012, p. 79)

Moreover, Puigvert (2012) makes a case for the following:

> A new modernity, a dialogic modernity, which contrasts with the traditional understanding, as well as it does with structuralist and poststructuralist perspectives. The dialogic turn in the social sciences is a result of an extension of dialogue in society, and an opportunity to counter neoliberalism. (p. 79)

As a part of her work with Latinx border populations and dialogic feminism, Cervantes-Soon (2012) recommends the incorporation of *testimonios* as a part of dialogic approaches. *Testimonios* originated in Latin American, indigenous, emancipatory struggles, calling attention to painful events or series of oppressions and recognition of indigenous peoples' knowledge (Mench´u, 1984; Smith, 2005). Accordingly, "the *testimonio* becomes a means for agency" (Cervantes-Soon, 2012, p. 374). The narrator of the testimonio is no longer silent and is allowed to move beyond oppression, colonization, and patriarchy. Cervantes-Soon (2012) notes the following:

> *Testimonios* allow us to put the scattered pieces together of a painful experience in a new way that generates wisdom and consciousness; *testimonios* thus offer the opportunity to develop and expose theory in the flesh and urge the audience to action. (p. 374)

Subaltern women of color have also used *testimonios* to advance dialogic feminism and emancipatory goals. The Latina Feminist Group (2001) used *testimonios* to shed light and inform others of their complex identities while joining together to recognize problematic silence and isolation that serves to perpetuate oppression in their communities and in the academy.

Reilly (2011) argues for a commitment to processes of critically re-interpreting universal human rights, as part of the fabric of emancipatory forms of transnational feminism (Reilly, 2009), and that such forms are possible in the confluence of the following interdependent conditions:

- a critical feminist global consciousness that challenges the systemic interplay of oppressive patriarchal, capitalist and racist power relations across multiple flexible boundaries locally and transnationally;

- practical engagement with mainstream human rights that continually contests its hegemonic concepts and practices in ways that extend the application of human rights to previously excluded and/or marginalized individuals, groups, issues, and contexts;
- recognition of the intersectionality of women's identities and experiences across multiple categories and a commitment to reciprocal, cross-boundaries dialogue in the formulation of any common agendas and actions, which such recognition demands;
- practical development of collaborative advocacy networks and strategies, above and below states, around concrete issues aimed at transforming conditions inimical to the substantive realization of human rights;
- ongoing engagement in global forums and decision-making arenas as sites of transnational solidarity and citizenship (Reilly, 2011, p. 62).

Reilly (2011) puts forth the need for counter-hegemonic approaches to human rights that reassert the social, economic, and cultural rights within both public and private domains. Hegemony dictates human rights from Western-defined, neoliberal lenses. Discourses within this hegemonic framework disseminate universal interpretations what constitutes human needs and hopes. However, this universalization of human rights is based on "processes of Westernization and modernization, the reproduction of a false hierarchy of 'the West' and 'the rest' and the justification of imposing Western-defined agendas . . . in the name of promoting rights" (Reilly, 2011, p. 64). In many cases, these Western perspectives conflict with an emancipatory understanding of human rights. Ultimately the roles of the liberal public institutions and private domains in perpetuating gender inequalities must be challenged. Both state-sponsored and private sphere violations of civil and political rights must be considered as human rights issues.

As public institutions lose government funding and support the human experience is mediated through increasingly disjointed, incongruent, and distanced technology-influenced forms of home, work, social, and cultural life, considerations for human rights are devalued. Reilly (2011) recommends the development of a unified confrontation of the following:

> different but linked effects of neoliberal globalization in women's lives. If it is to emerge, to be emancipatory it must employ an intersectional lens that recognizes the cumulative advantages experienced by some women in relatively privileged locations within the global political-cultural economy and the corollary of intersectional or cumulative disadvantages experienced by others. (pp. 73–74)

Reilly (2011, p. 74) recommends unified alliances, but cautions against the "false" universalization of women's causes, and notes "universal principles or the possibility of common cause appear to have missed a key point about the role that universal claims can play in shaping emancipatory possibility." False universalization, women's differences, intersections of oppression, and privilege are part of emancipatory dialogic feminism around which new solidarities might be negotiated (Mohanty, 2003; Yuval-Davis, 2006). Mohanty (2003), Yuval-Davis (2006), and Reilly (2011) encourage a contemplation of how to do women's human rights' in emancipatory ways. Counter-hegemonic discourses and activities should challenge universals while, at the same time, facilitate acts of solidarity in which the contents of women's human rights are created by those who were previously excluded.

Chapter 5

Transnational Possibilities

The Importance of Critical Cosmopolitanism and Pragmatic Hope

INTRODUCTION

Productive dialogue across geographic, socioeconomic, historical, and psychological borders is contingent on critical cosmopolitanism and, ultimately, pragmatic hope. Critical cosmopolitanism is an emerging direction in social theory and reflects both an object of study and a distinctive methodological approach to the social world. It differs from normative political and moral accounts of cosmopolitanism as world polity or universalistic culture in its conception of cosmopolitanism as socially situated and as part of the self-constituting nature of the social world itself. It is an approach that shifts the emphasis to internal developmental processes from viewing globalization as the primary mechanism for cosmopolitanism. This signals a post-universalistic kind of cosmopolitanism, which is not merely a condition of diversity but is articulated in cultural models of world openness through which societies undergo transformation (Delanty, 2006, p. 25).

Critical cosmopolitanism provides a pathway to hope. Pragmatic hope relates to meliorism, faith, and social progress and is rooted in pragmatism (Shade, 2001). Stitzlein (2019) argues that pragmatic hope seeks to revive hope that is grounded in real struggles. This hope serves as an outgrowth of philosophical pragmatism, which, in turn, is related to experiences and agency connected to democratic participation.

CRITICAL COSMOPOLITANISM

According to Delanty (2006), "Cosmopolitanism became linked with the universalism of modern western thought and with political designs aimed at world governance" (2006, p. 26). Much of the recent and current body of academic work focuses on cosmopolitan political theory rather than social theory (Cohen, 1996; Lu, 2000; Vertovec & Cohen, 2002; Tan, 2004). There has been an "implication that cosmopolitanism was equated with the political in opposition to the social" (Delanty, 2006). In other words, cosmopolitans have been viewed as citizens of the world who reject narrow world-views. Cosmopolitanism includes concepts like de-nationalization, transnationalization, network, scapes, and interconnectedness. Yet, Beck (2009) argues for something that supercedes traditional and historical cosmopolitanism, cosmopolitan realism. Cosmopolitan realism contrasts with cosmopolitan idealism. This approach promotes a recognition and restitution for past wrongs that are the root causes of current issues, including "the consequences of colonialism, the slave system, the holocaust (Beck, 2009, pp. 22–23).

Beck (2009) recommends taking a stand against the "cosmopolitan myth that life between frontiers or in the diaspora automatically implies greater openness to the world" (p. 23). On the contrary, cosmopolitan realism holds that the inner cosmopolitanization of nationally conceived and organized societies also increases the likelihood of a national false fabrication of facts and data. Cultural differences can invalidate universalized codes and meanings that some academic researchers depend on. This problematic situation provides a realization and justification for research methodologies more aligned with critical cosmopolitanism. Traditional cosmopolitanism has been used to justify wars and expanding military budgets (Delanty, 2006). In a similar manner, simply being concerned with promoting a diverse, global marketplace promotes false claims of cosmopolitan diversity. Cosmopolitanism is considered an "outlook toward the challenges and opportunities of being a person or community dwelling in a world of ongoing social transformation" (Hansen et al., 2009, p. 587). According to Hansen et al., cosmopolitanism is

> the ever-changing space between what a person and community are in the present moment and what they might become through a reflective response to new influence juxtaposed with an understanding of their traditions and roots. Terms like cosmopolitan orientation, outlook, and way of life capture this viewpoint. Cosmopolitanism as we understand it gives rises to modes of sustaining individual and community integrity in the face of unrelenting influences from the world. (2009, p. 588)

Political, moral, cultural, and economic cosmopolitanism (Kleingeld & Brown, 2006) are vital responses to the aforementioned needs of listening to and respecting the disempowered. Delanty (2006) puts forth the need for a rejection of traditional cosmopolitanism. In accordance with this refutation, the dominant notion of cosmopolitanism as social theory should be replaced as follows:

> Current developments in social theory suggest a post-universalistic cosmopolitanism that takes as its point of departure different kinds of modernity and processes of societal transformation that do not presuppose the separation of the social from the political or postulate a single world culture. (p. 27)

Delanty (2006) refers to critical cosmopolitanism as social theory and approaches characterized by valuing internal development over globalization. Critical cosmopolitan social theory rejects earlier kinds of cosmopolitanism and does not embrace singular, western ideas of modernity and globalization. Critical cosmopolitanism refers to "the multiplicity of ways in which the social world is constructed in different modernities" (Delanty, 2006, p. 27). World openness is an important component of critical cosmopolitanism. Additionally, social transformation is promoted rather than tenets of universalism. Delanty (2006) also put forth the following:

> Critical cosmopolitanism concerns the analysis of cultural modes of mediation by which the social world is shaped and where the emphasis is on moments of world openness created out of the encounter of the local with the global. (p. 27)

The notion of hybridity plays a prominent role in cultural approaches to globalization, yet hybridity does not fully account for cosmopolitanism (Delanty, 2006). Societies and cultures have developed distinctly through processes of syncretism whereby different elements are combined to produce something new. Cross-fertilization of cultures also occurs in contemporary societies, hybridity can be associated with cross-cultural communities that resist cosmopolitanism as they are societies that resist universal norms. Thus, hybridity can be an important component of cosmopolitanism, but "it is not itself the defining feature" (Delanty, 2006, p. 33).

As opposed to traditional cosmopolitanism, critical cosmopolitanism accommodates what is deemed local, provincial, or less worldly. What takes place within the processes of critical cosmopolitanism is "an internal cognitive transformation" and "a developmental change in the social world arising out of competing cultural models" (Delanty, 2006, p. 40). According to Delanty (2006), there are three main dimensions of cosmopolitanism:

1. the historical level of modernity,
2. the macro or societal level of the interaction of societies or societal systems, and
3. the micro level of identities, movements and communities within the social world (p. 40).

Critical cosmopolitanism proceeds on the assumption that learning takes place within cultures and possibilities exist for the development of societies. Moreover, critical cosmopolitanism plays a role "in opening up discursive spaces of world openness and thus in resisting both globalization and nationalism" (Delanty, 2006, p. 44).

Cosmopolitanism processes generate paradoxes in that individuals may develop and reinforce their consciousness of the influences of home cultures and personal values. On the other hand, cosmopolitanism should restructure culture and values so that there is an inclusiveness of disempowered humanity's perspectives, understandings, activities, and insights.

Hansen et al. (2009) argue for a critical cosmopolitanism that provides bottom-up as opposed to top-down educational responses to challenges with regard to the present human condition. According to Hansen et al. (2009),

> Hope, memory, and dialogue are substantive arts that can be cultivated through education and which, when exercised in concert with other persons, can give people strength to hold their doors open, to let what Gandhi called free air circulate. (2009, pp. 606–607)

PRAGMATIC HOPE

Critical cosmopolitanism and efficacious transborder dialogue, offer pragmatic hope. Koopman (2006) describes pragmatism "as a philosophical way of taking hope seriously" (p. 106). Pragmatism develops the philosophical resources of hope. Accordingly, traditional philosophical concepts are reconstructed through pragmatic visions.

Meliorism is a key component of pragmatism, and the value of meliorism within pragmatist constructs is noted by Koopman (2006). Pragmatist meliorism and hope encourage a renewal of society and counters the prevailing conditions. Moreover, democratic hope serves as the critical philosophical advance put forth by pragmatism (Koopman, 2006).

According to Shade (2006), "A pragmatic approach to hope will share this general understanding but give special attention to the actual but problematic conditions that generate specific hopes" (p. 194). An essential component of hope is that it functions to provide possible resolutions, or paths to resolutions, for problems. Realization of these ends requires an intelligent assessment of real conditions and requisite means for resolutions. Shade (2006) reasons that hope "involves a dialectical consideration of the desirability and realizability of its ends, thereby giving us a basis for distinguishing hoping from wishing and other fantastical ways of thinking that lack realizable grounds" (p. 195). Habits are a key consideration, as a pragmatic view of hope articulates the vital roles of habits as part of feats. Rather than be mindless, repetitive actions, habits should be "dispositions we develop through our interaction with the environment; they are abilities that arise from successful transactions, generating pathways of promising, productive activities" (Shade, 2006, p. 195). Habit, therefore, becomes a way of organizing our strengths and deeds to offer possibilities for fruitful actions.

Reflection is a key component of effective habits and pragmatic hope. Dewey (1910) describes reflective thinking as "the kind of thinking that consists in turning a subject over in the mind and giving it serious and consecutive consideration. . . . It enables us to know what we are about when we act. It converts action which is merely appetitive, blind, and impulsive into intelligent action" (p. 125). Intelligent action brought together knowledge and experience and made the connection between reflective thinking and associated communication in the creation of meaning from experience. Reflection allowed for an experience "to be formulated in order to be communicated. To formulate requires getting outside of it, seeing it as another would see it, considering what points of contact it has with the life of another so that it may be got into such form that he can appreciate its meaning" (1916, p. 8).

Intelligent habits "are the seat of our agency and the basis of growth and meaningful activity" (Shade, 2006, p. 195). For hopes to be realized, as opposed to hope that results in futility, pragmatic hope examines and addresses problematic situations as well as how those problems can be solved. Pragmatic hope also requires habits of persistence, resourcefulness, courage and should play an important role in school curricula (Shade, 2006). As such Shade puts forth,

> A hopeful pedagogy can guide the development of our children's capacity to hope through modeling and acquiring hope's habits. To the extent that habits of persistence, resourcefulness and courage are needed to learn basic skills, hope blends naturally with the curriculum. Special attention to these habits helps students see how hope can assist them in overcoming obstacles and securing desired goods. As they face their own challenges in the classroom, teachers are in a prime position to serve as role-models of hopeful behavior. They can also design cooperative activities among students that extend agency and foster trust and connection. (Shade, 2006, p. 222)

Hopeful responses to poverty and violence as these problems affect students' home and educational experiences must include collective agency and student participation in decision-making processes that address their concerns. According to Shade (2006), pragmatic hope "is an even more valuable resource when the larger community commits to cultivating and protecting habits of hope; without such measures, debilitating external circumstances may more readily spill over into and negatively affect the classroom" (Shade, 2006, p. 223). Hope prevails when community approaches to violence protect our children by involving the community in the life of the school. Resources and coordinated efforts are necessary pre-requisites for the amelioration of the grim conditions that foster poverty and violence. A key reason for embracing a pragmatic hope "is that it focuses our attention on both individual and communal habits needed" (Shade, 2006, p. 223).

In this manner, pragmatic hope can be a constructive approach for students, teachers, and the community. It also offers hope for preventing, addressing, and correcting circumstances that currently serve as barriers to educational processes and successes. Freire (2005) described educational praxis as reflection and action taken to transform the world. Accordingly, transformation entails understanding and challenging a world marked by inequality and oppressive power relations. Stanger (2018) refers to a "pedagogy of hope" (p. 49) and "praxis through which a sense of embodied community and hopeful self-definition is built in resistance to racist, sexist and neoliberal discourses that serve to pathologize" (p. 60).

Grass roots, critical cosmopolitanism combined with pragmatic hope offer possibilities for widened understandings, educational change, and policy making. This combination of critical cosmopolitanism and pragmatic hope must include indigenous and de-colonized perspectives. In this manner, hegemonic, top-down decision making can be affected and countered within our educational, governmental, and economic institutions. Productive and effective transborder dialogue is a requisite first step as we move down this path. From that initial position, our society can proceed with more informed and enlightened transborder pedagogies.

Chapter 6

Navigating the Intersection of Border Pedagogy and Critical Place-Based Pedagogies[*]

INTRODUCTION

This chapter explicates the intersection of place-based and border pedagogies, including how transnational, comparative studies and issues-centered pedagogies are central to understanding one's own situatedness. Place-based and border pedagogies provide a platform for effectively crossing borders inherent to larger research, intellectual knowledge, appreciation, and learning. Critical border dialogism engages educators, cultural workers, and policy makers in a multiplicity of discourses and interchange. Voices, in turn, represent positionalities embedded in place-based and border discourses. Critical border dialogism (Cashman, 2015) is a process that resituates teachers, students, cultural workers, decision makers, policy makers, and the larger community. In this manner, common assumptions, practices, and judgments are challenged.

A critical border dialogism considers the interconnectness of place-based and border pedagogies as part of contemplating one's own positionality in the context of larger research, intellectual knowledge, appreciation, and learning (Cashman, 2015). According to Apple (2004), we are living at a time when critical education is discouraged. Given this current educational climate, the oppression educators feel is real, systemic, and structural (Apple, 2004). The power of that oppression is intensely felt in educational institutions and in educators' daily lives. According to Apple (2004), society must consider how to educate "future teachers so they are prepared to go forth and continue the process of building an education that resists incorporation into dominant forms" (p. 166) of oppression. The disenfranchisement and powerlessness of

---

[*] Content in this chapter was also published as: Cashman, T. G. (2016). Navigating the intersection of place-based pedagogy and border pedagogy: Resituating our positions through dialogic understandings. *International Journal of Critical Pedagogy*, 7(1), 29–50.

students, family members, educators, and cultural workers serve to confirm a sense of urgency for a critical border dialogism of teaching and learning. The concepts of heteroglossia (Abraham, 2014; Bakhtin, 1975/1981; Clark & Holquist, 1984; Holquist, 2002), meliorism (James, 1906; Kliebard, 2004; Koopman, 2006), critical cosmopolitanism (Mignolo, 2000a; Nouzeilles & Mignolo, 2003), nepantla (Abraham, 2014; Anzaldúa, 2002; Maffie, 2007; Mignolo, 2000b), dialogic feminism (Puigvert, 2012; Yaeger, 1991), and pragmatic hope (Koopman, 2006; Nolan & Stitzlein, 2011; Rorty, 1999; Shade, 2001) form the basis of the conditions for a critical border dialogic understanding of teaching and learning. Critical border dialogism offers hope for the reconstructionist approaches that are needed to address the structural inequities in our present-day schools. Specifically, as noted by Bowles and Gintis (1976), the internal organization of schools corresponds to the internal organization of a capitalist society's workforce in its structures, norms, and values according to the correspondence principle. In this manner, hierarchal control in schools reflects the structure of the market economy. Bowles and Gintis (2011) call for change based on the goals of economic democracy, as other methods of educational reform merely reproduce the old power relationships in new forms. Accordingly, diverse students of lower socioeconomic status have been systematically subjugated by the dominant class. Fragmented forms of consciousness are the result of this subjugation. In the United States, this fragmentation of consciousness and lack of unity is facilitated by racial, ethnic, sexual, gender, and socioeconomic antagonisms and exasperated by the dominant class as a form of dividing and conquering (Bowles & Gintis, 2011). This work is an explication of how critical border dialogism offers possibilities for challenging power relationships by underscoring its theoretical underpinnings in heteroglossia, meliorism, critical cosmopolitanism, nepantla, dialogic feminism, and pragmatic hope. Before conducting this explication, I offer a definition of critical border dialogism, exploring its intersections with place-based and border pedagogies and its philosophical underpinnings.

THE PEDAGOGICAL AND PHILOSOPHICAL UNDERPINNINGS OF CRITICAL BORDER DIALOGISM

Pedagogy is comprised of teaching and theories and debates related to teaching and learning, including analyses of the purposes of education, the nature of childhood and learning, and how knowledge is developed. Pedagogy engages educators in discourses interdependent on the act of teaching and the process of making sense of one's teaching (Alexander, 2009). Place-based and border pedagogical traditions, along with a reconstructionist philosophy of education form the foundation of critical border dialogism.

The Roles of Place-Based Pedagogies

Place-based pedagogies provide opportunities for students of various backgrounds to reflect on their positionalities and situatedness. Gruenewald (2003) argues that a pedagogy of place promotes understandings of social and ecological places. By incorporating critical approaches into place-based pedagogies, "we challenge the assumptions, practices, and outcomes taken for granted in dominant culture and in conventional education" (Gruenewald, 2003, p. 3). Gruenewald's critical pedagogy of place, therefore, links pedagogy of place with critical theory. A critical pedagogy of place stands in contrast with the survival-of-the-fittest educational philosophy that currently prevails in much of the United States. In the present educational environment, local considerations are eclipsed by discourses of accountability and economic competiveness (Gruenewald, 2003).

The Roles of Border Pedagogy

Border pedagogy, like a critical pedagogy of place, includes a concern for illuminating the spaces we occupy. Border pedagogy builds upon critical understandings of place and attempts to connect those understandings with larger contexts. According to Giroux (2005), there are three components of border pedagogy that indicate a respect for differences: (a) a recognition of margins, (b) the need for border crossers, and (c) a recognition of the historically and socially constructed strengths and limitations of places and borders. Borders are considered boundaries of entities, while the act of crossing borders involves going beyond existing boundaries and broadening one's perspectives of others in locales near or afar. Border pedagogy seeks to develop democratic education that respects the notion of difference as part of a common struggle to extend the quality of public life. It takes into consideration an "acknowledgement of shifting borders that both undermine and reterritorialize different configurations of culture, power, and knowledge" (Giroux, 2005, p. 20). Border pedagogy serves as a reconceptualization of existing ideologies and offers opportunities for students to engage the multiple references that constitute different cultural codes, experiences, and languages (Giroux, 2005). Border crossing educators contemplate their own belief systems, including understandings of their own pedagogy, biases, and limits (Giroux, 2005). Through border pedagogy, it is possible to recognize and contemplate the historical contexts of our differences. The concept of border pedagogy reveals diverse cultural histories and spaces to educators and their students. As stakeholders in educational processes, teachers and students traverse languages, experiences, and voices and undergo changes in their own personal identities (Giroux, 2005). Border pedagogy facilitates these transformations as students, teachers, administrators, and other cultural workers begin to recognize the multilayered and contradictory ideologies that construct their own identities. By acknowledging what comprises their individualities, educators and their students are better positioned to critically reflect on how theory is resituated in practice.

Transitioning to a Reconstructionist Philosophy of Education

The intersection of a critical pedagogy of place and border pedagogy serves to further the goals of reconstructionist education. According to Ornstein (2011), the philosophical base for reconstructionism is pragmatism. The instructional objective of both pragmatism and meliorism is to improve and reconstruct society. The knowledge base for reconstructionism includes skills and subjects need to identify and ameliorate problems of society (Ornstein, 2011). A reconstructionist believes in education for change and social reform. Learning is active and concerned with contemporary and future society. The teacher serves as an agent of change and reform. The teacher's role is also to act as a facilitator and research leader. Educators provide an environment for students to become aware of problems confronting humankind. The curriculum is designed to promote equality of education, cultural pluralism, understandings of international education, and futurism. There is an emphasis on individual growth and development. The individual has the opportunity to serve as a change agent, or one who has the ability to modify, even reconstruct the social environment (Ornstein, 2011). The attributes of a reconstructionist philosophy support critical pedagogy of place and border pedagogy in that reconstructionist philosophical approaches are dynamic, pragmatic, melioristic, and critical processes for examining and re-examining places and border spaces. Reconstructionism places an emphasis on the whole child, and students are actively engaged in their learning and develop meaning for their personal experiences and prior histories (Ornstein, 2011). Critical place-based pedagogies and border pedagogy follow on reconstructionist ideals as both pedagogical approaches provide spaces for learners to examine larger questions and issues. The traditional roles of teachers and students are overturned as all become one in the learning processes. Through this engagement in critical dialogism, participants reconstruct their own personal models of a just society and worldwide humanity. Critical border dialogism is the intersection of critical place-based pedagogies and border pedagogies. Critical border dialogism follows pragmatic, reconstructionist tenets that society can be deconstructed, improved, and reconstructed through effective dialogue. In the field of education, critical border dialogism informs those who seek to teach and learn as border crossers and problem solvers. Critical border dialogism works to develop broader visions and worldviews that resituate teachers, students, cultural workers, decision makers, policy makers, and the larger community and, in turn, clarifies a critical border praxis. The following section explicates the key theoretical precepts of critical border dialogism. Dynamic, reconstructionist curricula can be designed and facilitated by educators informed through critical border dialogism. Both critical border dialogism and critical border praxis, or the implementation of critical border dialogism, are extensions of border pedagogy and pedagogy of place with theoretical foundations based on (1) heteroglossia, (2) meliorism, (3) critical cosmopolitanism, (4) nepantla, (5) dialogic feminism, and (6) pragmatic hope. Through a critical border dialogism educators and cultural workers engage in complicated conversations of how to deconstruct, reconstruct, and ultimately further educational and societal goals. Under the following six subheadings, I explicate the theoretical backgrounds of heteroglossia, meliorism, critical cosmopolitanism, nepantla, dialogic feminism, and pragmatic hope.

Heteroglossia

Critical border dialogism, specifically its dialogic nature, is influenced by Mikhail Bakhtin's concept of heteroglossia, or multiple voices and utterances in a given context, as heteroglossia counters any sort of unilateral and unidirectional voices. Bakhtin argued for an interaction between the mind and the world (Holquist, 2002) and was influenced by his understandings of Kant. Kant's ideas fused sensibility and understanding as a form of knowledge. Bakhtin's ideas shifted to an emphasis on particularity and situatedness. Holquist (2002) maintained these positions, along with Bakhtin's underscoring the importance of understanding more abstract questions of selfhood, which should be considered within the context of location and place, including positionality. Bakhtin positioned dialogism as an epistemology. For Bakhtin, the key to understanding dualisms between the self and the other involved a simultaneous considering of same and different with relation to time and space. Accordingly, separateness and simultaneity are intrinsic to dialogue (Holquist, 2002). In The Dialogic Imagination, Bakhtin (1975/1981) articulated the concept of heteroglossia as "the base condition governing the operation of meaning in any utterance" (p. 263). The context of an utterance takes preeminence over the actual words uttered. As words uttered in a particular place and time have meanings different than under any other conditions; all utterances are "heteroglot" (p. 263). According to Bakhtin (1975/1981), the world is dominated by heteroglossia, and dialogism is a key characteristic of heteroglossia. According to Bakhtin, individual voices connect with other voices through dialogue (Clark & Holquist, 1984), and there is a constant interaction among meanings. All meanings have the potential to influence other meanings. People in positions of power over others seek to enforce a unitary language. Gramsci also critiqued the social norms and social structures that established and reinforced a unitary language (Gramsci et al., 1971). Gramsci's theory of cultural hegemony held that social, political, and economic dominance is preserved through systemic control and influence. Although Bakhtin's and Gramsci's positions differed on particular issues, both took issue with positivist social science and linguistics and developed their own anti-positivist theories (Brandist, 2006). In *Toward a Philosophy of the Act*, Bakhtin (1993) argues that we, as individuals, occupy places as a "being." No other person has occupied that same space simultaneously, and what is done by that person "can never be done by anyone else" (p. 40). This singularity of being provides for unique perspectives and positionality that cannot be claimed by another person. Bakhtin's work has driven the creation of a dialogic pedagogy (Matusov, 2009). A key aspect of that dialogic pedagogy is ideological becoming, or how a person becomes a unique individual. Thoughts form the foundation for our being and doing. Thoughts, in turn, are based on our discursive exchanges (Abraham, 2014). The focal point of ideological becoming is the meeting place between authoritative discourses and heteroglossia. Bakhtin (1975/1981) defined authoritative discourse as a discourse that "demands that we acknowledge it, that we make it our own; it binds us, quite independent of any power it might have to persuade us internally; we encounter it with its authority already fused to it" (p. 342). Authoritative discourse seeks to establish the hegemony of one ideology. An authoritative discourse "remains sharply demarcated, compact and inert; it deems, so to speak, not only quotation marks but a demarcation even more magisterial, a special script, for instance" (p. 343). On the other hand, heteroglot voices "pull against this centralization of thought and normalized ideology and only one way to mean" (Abraham, 2014, p. 11). Heteroglossia, moreover, serves as a complex mixture of languages, communications, and world views that is always "dialogized, as each language is viewed from the perspective of the others" (Dimitriadis & Kamberelis, 2006, p. 51). Dialogue is inherently heteroglot and juxtaposes ideas from various sources and time periods. Bakhtin (1975/1981) called heteroglossia the place where "real language lives" (p. 292) and also said that it is positioned uncompromisingly to counter official discourses. More specifically, heteroglossia includes languages that disturb others, languages that are deemed incorrect, and languages that are disregarded. Individuals are influenced by both authoritative discourses and heteroglossia (Bakhtin, 1975/1981). Authoritative discourses and heteroglossia are ever present in our lives through informal discussions, pop culture, the mainstream media, literary works, creative performances, film, and other forms of communication. Bakhtin calls for an awareness of the internally persuasive discourses that develop from both authoritative discourses and heteroglossia. Subliminally, these discourses have become embedded in a person's way of thinking. Discourse is not simply "information, directions, rules, models, and so forth-but strives rather to determine the very bases of our ideological interrelations with the world, the very basis of our behavior; it performs here as authoritative discourse, and an internally persuasive discourse" (p. 342). In Bakhtin's *Toward a Philosophy of the Act*, the concept of "being" is described as occupying a place that is "unique and never repeatable, a place that cannot be taken by anyone else and is impenetrable for anyone else" (Bakhtin, 1993, p. 40). From this state of being emerges the individual voice, the voice that contributes to discourse.

Heteroglossia is a concept that denounces authoritative, unilateral ideologies. Clark and Holquist (1984) maintain that Bakhtin's heteroglossia represents an ideal condition that safeguards against the hegemony of one-dimensional languages of truth or official positions in education and society.

Meliorism

If heteroglossia serves as the basis for dialogic principles, then social meliorism is key to the contemplation of why critical border dialogism is a requisite in an age of never-ending wars and conflict. Social meliorism combines pluralism with humanism and serves as the thesis that we are capable of creating better worlds and selves. Moreover, social meliorists believe education is a tool to restructure society and promote social change. This socialization goal is based on the power of the individual's intelligence and the ability to improve on intelligence through education (Kliebard, 2004). An individual's future is not predetermined by gender, race, socioeconomic status, heredity, or any other factors. Meliorism is the thesis that we are capable of improving the human condition. Confidence and exerted efforts are integral to meliorism (James, 1906). Melioristic confidence offers a genuine alternative to the dualistic natures of pessimism and optimism (Koopman, 2006). Social meliorism provides constructs for educational researchers, teachers, students, and cultural workers so they can deliberate on how to improve societal conditions. Social meliorism enhances educational systems by incorporating models, practices, innovations, and attributes of other educational systems in the context of comparative, international, and transnational investigations (Wilson, 2003). In summation, social meliorism is central to effective pedagogies and at the core of all critical border dialogism.

Critical Cosmopolitanism

Critical cosmopolitanism incorporates elements of social meliorism as it is an argument bettering society. The important role of critical cosmopolitanism as part of critical border dialogism is that it provides voices from the populous and serves as a defense of globalization from below. Critical cosmopolitanism also argues for the geopolitical diversal. Critical cosmopolitanism differs from cosmopolitanism as critical cosmopolitan social theory explicates the multiple ways in which the social world is constructed (Delanty, 2006). Mignolo (2000a) reasoned that cosmopolitanism was conceived from those with local histories positioned to devise and enact global designs. Other local histories, in turn, were influenced by those global designs. For that reason, cosmopolitanism today has to become critical, border-thinking, and dialogic and from the perspective of those local histories affected by global designs (Mignolo, 2000a). Diversity is considered a universal and cosmopolitan project and is the focus of critical and dialogic cosmopolitanism. In this manner, authoritative discourses are replaced by diversality. According to Kincheloe (2008), "Diversality connotes the dire need for different perspectives" and "for multiple forms of knowledge" (p. 3). Kincheloe asserted that European heritage, Christianity, and western philosophical approaches take precedence over other cultures, and other forms of knowledge, including indigenous knowledge, are not placed on equal footing. Kincheloe referred to diversal knowledges as insights from different locales and representations of a variety of worldviews. All of these worldviews add to our understanding of world dynamics, including human suffering. These diversal knowledges augment "our ability to imagine new ways of seeing and being and interacting with other people and the physical world" (p. 5). Mignolo (2000a) also argued for diversality as a universal project and for border thinking as a necessary epistemology upon which critical cosmopolitanism shall be articulated in a postnational world order governed by global capitalism and new forms of coloniality. Mignolo argued for a bottom-up approach to cosmopolitanism, as opposed to the current top-down hierarchy. Accordingly, "it is an argument for globalization from below; at the same time, it is an argument for the geopolitically diversal" (p. 744). Critical cosmopolitanism is seen as a medium of societal transformation that is based on the principle of world interconnectedness. Critical cosmopolitanism also promotes societal change by encouraging self-reflection and self-transformation, in the hopes of developing new cultural forms and new discourses. Critical cosmopolitanism has a "critical role to play in opening up discursive spaces of world openness and thus in resisting both globalization and nationalism" (p. 44). Critical cosmopolitanism provides us with a viable option to the ever-present neo-positivism that surrounds educational systems in the twenty-first century. This neo-positivism is characterized by reduction; reduction is undertaken through an analysis of meanings and subsequent diminution to their simplest statements. In a time of test-driven curricula, critical cosmopolitanism is an educational approach that questions neo-positivism, reductionism, dualism, and paternalism. Thus, critical cosmopolitanism serves as an essential component of critical border dialogism. Movement along the path of diversality and empowerment from below are crucial cogs in the wheels of critical border praxis, or the follow-up and execution of principles intrinsic to critical border dialogism.

Nepantla

Critical border dialogism is influenced by indigenous knowledge that crosses multiple conditions of borders. "Nepantla," as a form of indigenous knowledge, is a key part of the dialogue indispensable for critical border praxis. Nepantla is a word that originated in the Nahuatl language, the lingua franca of the indigenous Nahua in Mexico and Central America (Anzaldúa, 1987; Maffie, 2007). Nepantla serves as a form of indigenous knowledge that places people and things within surroundings characterized by dynamism, fluidity, and the possibilities for social transformation. Anzaldúa (1987) defined nepantla as bridges that cross liminal spaces to connect worlds. Abraham (2014) maintained that the Nahua held perspectives of a world characterized by elements of disorder, the process of becoming, and flexibility or transitions. Maffie (2007) stated that historically, nepantla was the part of how the Nahua envisioned the world and is rooted in a belief system that places people and cultural objects within "a dynamic zone of mutual transaction, confluence, unstable and diffuse identity, and transformation" (p. 16). Mignolo (2000b) argued that the Nahua developed nepantla as a consciousness in response to their encounter and subsequent ideological and physical domination by Spanish conquistadors invaders, and missionaries. Maffie (2007) spoke of nepantla as being a process that is "dialectical, transitional, and oscillating; centering as well as destabilizing; and abundant with mutuality and reciprocity" (p. 11). Nepantla is simultaneously destructive and creative, and it is also "transformative" (p. 11). Abraham (2014) linked Anzaldúa's nepantla to Bakhtin's ideological becoming. Nepantla leads us to question physical, linguistic, social, and cultural borders. Both nepantla and the notion of becoming are theoretical stances that put forth that we, as humans, are in a continual process of forming ideas and that those ideas are influenced by historical and current discourses (Abraham, 2014). Educators may be applying the worldviews espoused in nepantla in today's classrooms through red pedagogy (Grande, 2004). Red pedagogy is based, in part, on the following argument for decolonized education: The ongoing injustices of the world call educators-as-students-as-activists to work together—to be in solidarity as we work to change the history of empire and struggle in the common project of decolonization. To do so requires courage, humility, and love (Grande, 2004, p. 175). Red pedagogy brings a realization and consideration for sovereignty and living out active presences and "survivances." Grande (2004) described survivances as native renunciations of dominance, tragedy, and victimry. The survivance narratives contemplate the "struggles of indigenous peoples and the lived reality of colonization as a complexity that extends far beyond the parameters of economic capitalist oppression" (p. 175). Grande (2004) put forth that scholars, educators, and students "must exercise critical consciousness" and create a new meeting place for "indigenous and nonindigenous peoples will work in solidarity to envision a way of life and replete with spirit" (p. 176). Critical border dialogism provides spaces for crossing the borders that were determined by dominant groups and offers opportunities for dialectical approaches to "otherness." Nepantla and red pedagogy provide educational systems and policy makers with counter-narratives in an age of high-stakes assessments, funding shortfalls for public education, and the creeping privatization of public education. Indigenous pedagogies that correspond with nepantla and red pedagogy challenge the neo-positivist beliefs of our current materialistic, consumerist society. Nepantla and red pedagogy offer hope for the repositioning of educators and cultural workers, so that they become empowered and better equipped to challenge dominant educational discourses.

Dialogic Feminism

Dialogic feminism is a necessary component of critical border dialogism as it upholds renunciation, resistance, and counter-hegemonic actions to patriarchy and gender violence in its many forms. Dialogic feminism uncovers the "complex, contorted play of hegemonic forms and female speech" and "explore the ways in which women from a variety of temporalities, ethnicities, races, and classes initiate dialogues with their oppressions" (Yaeger, 1991, p. 240). Through intersections of feminist practices and dialogic voices, the practice of dialogic feminism provides society with compelling narratives of power struggles. Moreover, feminist dialogics allows us to pinpoint and describe the dynamic changes within feminism itself (Yaeger, 1991). Emancipation is central to the process of becoming, and feminist dialogics, like nepantla, coincide with Bakhtin's concepts of ideological becoming. A movement toward dialogic understandings of societies and education has significance for the understanding of social groups, for the advancement of theory related to social groups, and for "how social sciences can inform the struggles of these groups and thus make a contribution to their own emancipation" (Puigvert, 2012, p. 89). When we, as educators and cultural workers, dismiss the role of dialogue in the analysis of societies and the possibility to transform them, "it means dismissing the capacity of citizens to reflect on society, analyze it, decide on it, and transform it" (Puigvert, 2012,

p. 93). Critical dialogism seeks to challenge and eliminate the patriarchy that still plagues public discourses on education, cross-border knowledge, and conflict resolution. Dialogic feminism, as an integral part of critical border dialogism, provides dialectal approaches within counter-hegemony. At the same time, dialogic feminism offers fresh analyses and courses of action within feminism. Yaeger (1991) cautions against normalizing categories, routines, and ideologies. Feminist dialogics can help us pinpoint and describe the dynamic changes within feminism itself (Yaeger, 1991). A dialogic feminism provides dynamic renunciation, resistance, and counter-hegemonic actions to patriarchy and other barriers in the feminist struggle. Dialogue in the public and private spheres can lead to a recognition and transformation of violence and aggression into dialogue and consensus. Dialogic relations are constructed through social consensus, which works in favor of reducing gender violence. Transformations in society, including our educational institutions, transpire when social agents intervene in existing unequal structures (Puigvert, 2012). Dialogic feminism provides us with opportunities for analyzing the contexts of dialogue and the subsequent redefining of social contexts (Puigvert, 2012). Productive discourses in educational settings are part of critical border dialogism, as critical border dialogism seeks to better address and problem-solve the roots of current conflicts. Conflict resolution emerges as a priority. Dialogue in the public and private spheres can lead to a recognition and transformation of violence and aggression. If, indeed, patriarchy is associated with various forms of violence, a dialogic feminism provides us with pragmatic hope for a society with members who are empowered to overcome patriarchy and its inherent violence. Through dialogic feminism we can better envision an educational system where the struggle for transformative knowledge takes precedence over competiveness. In this manner, formal education can move in the direction of struggle, solidarity, and community as central foci. These approaches stand in contrast to the survival-of-the-fittest tactics currently advocated and employed by policy makers such as high-stakes assessments. Rather, dialogic processes play a key role in more inclusive educational processes, and educational policies and discourses are less dominated by patriarchal voices.

Pragmatic Hope

Critical border dialogism is also comprised of pragmatic hope, as it encourages educators and cultural workers to confront the problems facing our educational systems through collective action. When we hope pragmatically we recognize the conflict embedded in social contexts and approach such struggles with thoughtful action (Shade, 2001). Pragmatism involves a willingness to live "without assurances or guarantees' (James, 1906, p.

124). True beliefs are sustained through actions taken by humans. Pragmatic hope, in turn, offers that we can make necessary changes in our society (Koopman, 2006). In the early twentieth century, James and Dewey replaced predestiny with hope in their writing and thinking (Rorty, 1999). Koopman (2006) connected pragmatic hope with democratic principles and argued that democratic hope is furthered through pragmatism. In the field of education, pragmatic hope provides educators with a greater sense of optimism. Through pragmatic hope teachers and administrators feel their voices can be heard and their efforts can be valued. Pragmatic hope re-energizes teachers, school administrators, and cultural workers. What emerges is a new conviction and a sensing of the possibilities for meaningful changes and improvement of conditions in our educational systems (Shade, 2001). Pragmatic hope, as it provides underlying support for the principles of critical border dialogism, opens up discourses on possible forms of responsible assessment. Given the current educational policies, including the current system of punishment and rewards based on the results of standardized tests, critical border dialogism and its pragmatic hope offer a mechanism for the examination of optional forms of appraisal (Nolan & Stitzlein, 2011). The current U.S. educational climate is characterized by increased anxiety and lowered morale among educators. In this context, pragmatic hope offers teachers, administrators, and cultural workers reasons for continuing their struggles. Ultimately, it is in the best interests of our society that educators are re-positioned as professionals who can imagine and take action toward improved alternatives. Conceptual tools should model and develop hope in preservice educators, classroom teachers, and future scholars.

Critical border dialogism, with pragmatic hope as its bulwark, calls for a confrontation of today's problems with reflection and collective action. As a short-term solution it offers possibilities for a transcendence of some of the limitations currently imposed on schools. For the longer term, pragmatic hope offers opportunities for the reconceptualization of schooling and reallocation of resources in public education. Although hope is tempered by anxiety and low morale under present schooling conditions, pragmatic hope can provide long-term approaches needed for a reconceptualization of what it is to teach and learn (Nolan & Stitzlein, 2011, p. 9).

THE CALL FOR CRITICAL BORDER DIALOGISM

As noted by Bowles and Gintis' (1976) in their correspondence principle and Bourdieu's (1977) social reproduction theory, social conditions have been created by self-serving hierarchal, corporate, and military-industrial-congressional complex interests in our present-day educational institutions.

Critical border dialogism offers the conviction that societal woes can, indeed, be addressed and ameliorated through quality educational experiences, we can draw upon successful models that exist beyond our own political, geographic, historical, and philosophical borders. We can build upon our existing knowledges of place and understandings of borders. Through dialectal approaches to education, we contemplate the multiplicity of voices, including the counter-hegemonic spaces of nepantla and dialogic feminism. Pragmatic hope offers a vision for the struggles that lay ahead for individuals and educational institutions that bridge local understandings with global interconnectedness. Critical border dialogism must consider the historical contexts of borders, border conflicts, the present and future development of transborder relations and regions and current border and transborder policies. Educators and cultural workers need to engage in dialogue on the impact of the historical contexts of border conflicts for societies. There must be a deliberation on the economic, cultural, and political ramifications of transborder migrations and interactions. The resultant formation and development of new border identities and regions needs special attention. Furthermore, the various features of border policies must be closely investigated for efficacy and sources of conflict. In terms of schools and the school curriculum, critical border

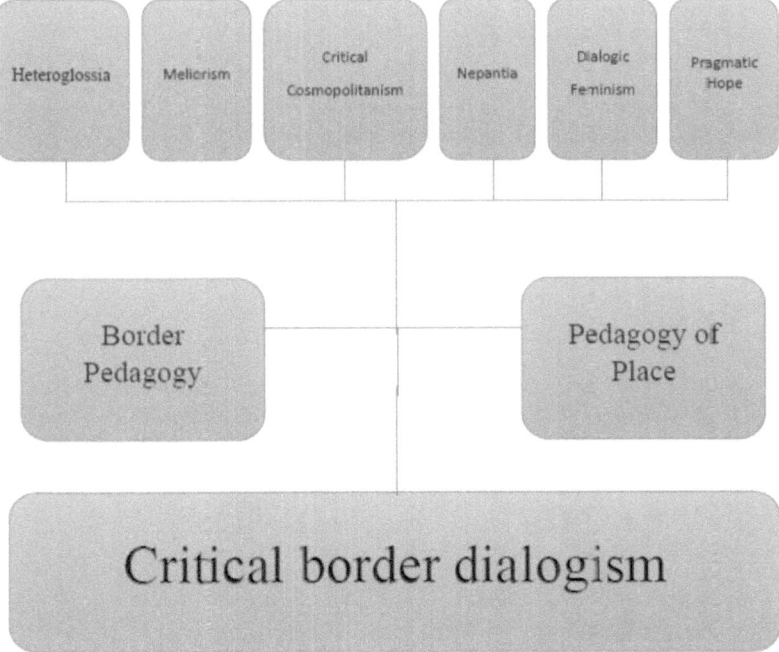

Figure 6.1 Theoretical Underpinnings of a Critical Border Dialogism.

dialogism and critical border praxis must engage professional educators and cultural workers in key roles of determining what gets included or omitted from curricula. This stands in contrast to present conditions where lobbyists, textbook publishers, corporate sponsors, and policy makers are responsible for key decisions regarding curricula. Critical border dialogism is the culmination of all of the concepts noted; moreover, it positions educators and cultural workers to engage in multidirectional discourses from (a) student to teacher, (b) teacher to student, (c) student to student, (d) teacher to teacher, (e) teacher to administrator, (f) administrator to teacher, (g) educator to policy maker, and (h) cultural worker to policy maker. Communication and decision making follow a more bottom-up pattern than a top-down, hierarchal policy-making model. Through critical border dialogism students, family members, educators, cultural workers, and policy makers serve as stakeholders. Critical border dialogism equips us with the tools to challenge common assumptions, practices, and judgments. Moreover, individuals are empowered to question and counter-hegemonic systems that dictate teaching and learning within our societies (see figure 6.1).

Chapter 7

Critical Border Praxis*

Choosing the Path

INTRODUCTION

This chapter explicates processes of transforming critical border dialogism into critical border praxis. Critical border dialogism resituates teachers, students, cultural workers, decision makers, policy makers, and the larger community and positions us, as educators, students, cultural workers, and members of the larger community, on the course to critical border praxis. Critical border praxis actively engages us as cross borders in a contemplation of historically and socially constructed limitations.

Critical border praxis is defined as the process of building a community of teachers and learners who are empowered and contribute to society through their sustained engagement in critical border dialogic processes. In this manner, educators, including administrators and teachers, and students are part of the process of becoming. Broader visions and worldviews inform and resituate teachers, students, cultural workers, decision makers, policy makers, and the larger community who, in turn, are empowered through critical border praxis. Effective transborder dialogue among stakeholders provides a foundation for this critical border praxis.

Pedagogy and Border Crossings

Alexander (2009) describes pedagogy, including pedagogy of place, as encompassing the act of teaching and related theories and debate. including analyses of the character of culture and society, the purposes of education, the nature

---

* Content in this chapter was also published as: Cashman, T. G. (2016). Critical border praxis: Choosing the path of critical border dialogism. *Critical Education*, 7(1), 1–16.

of childhood and learning, and the structure of knowledge. Pedagogy involves discourses related to the act of teaching and the process of analyzing the efficacy of teaching (Alexander, 2009). Gruenewald (2003) argues that pedagogy of place can be a means of examining the connections between individuals and their inhabited spaces. Place-based pedagogies promote understandings of social and ecological places. Critical, place-based approaches influence assumptions, practices, and outcomes. A critical pedagogy of place promotes pedagogical approaches that contrast with the discourses of accountability, standardized assessments, and economic competitiveness that prevail in the current U.S. educational environment (Gruenewald, 2003). Comparative, critical place-based pedagogies serve to continually provide educators with ways of building bridges across racial, ethnic, sexual, gender, and socioeconomic lines. In this manner, students of various backgrounds learn about their personal, local, and regional spaces and develop the confidence to make connections and to broaden their understandings of national and global environs. Gruenewald (2003) argues that pedagogy of place can be a means of examining the connections between individuals and their inhabited spaces. Place-based pedagogies promote understandings of social and ecological places. By incorporating critical approaches into place-based pedagogies, "we challenge the assumptions, practices, and outcomes taken for granted in dominant culture and in conventional education" (Gruenewald, 2003, p. 3). Border pedagogy, in turn, engages a critical pedagogy of place in its discourses. Border pedagogy builds upon critical understandings of place and attempts to connect those understandings with larger contexts. According to Giroux (2005), border pedagogy involves a recognition and understanding of margins as affected by history, power, and difference. Moreover, an individual must contemplate historically and socially constructed limitations to become a border crosser who has developed new understandings of others (Giroux, 2005). Borders are considered boundaries of entities, while the act of crossing borders entails going beyond existing boundaries and broadening one's perspectives of others in locales near or afar. In this manner, transnational studies that incorporate place-based pedagogy and border pedagogy promote respect for differences and, in turn, promote greater understandings of others.

Border pedagogy provides hope for democratic education that respects the notion of difference as part of a common struggle to extend the quality of public life. It takes into consideration an "acknowledgement of shifting borders that both undermine and reterritorialize different configurations of culture, power, and knowledge" (Giroux, 2005, p. 20). Border pedagogy serves as a reconceptualization of existing ideologies. Accordingly, border pedagogy is dynamic and includes the following components: (a) a recognition of epistemological, political, cultural, and social margins; (b) the need to create pedagogical conditions in which students become border crossers and understand otherness; and (c) the teaching and learning of historically and socially constructed borders that frame our discourses and social relations (Giroux, 2005). Border pedagogy offers the opportunity for students to engage the multiple references that constitute different cultural codes, experiences, and languages (Giroux, 2005). Teachers, in turn, are able to deepen their own understanding of the "limits, partiality, and particularity of their own politics, values, and pedagogy" (Giroux, 2005, p. 26). The concept of border pedagogy unwraps diverse cultural histories and spaces to educators and students. It is in border spaces where educational institutions and the larger society meet, where the relevancies between teachers and cultural workers come into play, and where schooling is understood within the larger realm of cultural politics. Multicentric perspectives allow teachers, cultural workers, and students to recognize the multiplicity of layers and contradictory ideologies that construct personal identities. Moreover, border pedagogy allows educators to also "analyze how the differences within and between various groups can expand the potential of human life and democratic possibilities" (Giroux, 2005, p. 151). It is important for educators, as cultural workers, to resituate theory in practice so students critically reflect on their voices and experiences. Students have an "obligation to interrogate the claims or consequences their assertions have for the social relationships they legitimate" (Giroux, 2005, p. 152). Border pedagogy also offers students "the opportunity to engage the multiple references and codes that position them within various structures of meaning and practice" (Giroux, 2005, p. 152). Critical border pedagogy considers borders as dynamic inhabited regions rather than divided, disparate locales divided by a political boundary (Reyes & Garza, 2005). The U.S. and Mexico borderlands serve as fluid and connected sociopolitical zones (Romo & Chavez, 2006). Romo and Chavez argue that the geopolitical border of Mexico and the United States represents a transition zone and blending of languages, cultures, communities, and countries. Moreover, the U.S. and Mexico borderlands reflect "the complexity, juxtaposition, and intersection of identities, economies, and social and educational issues" (Romo & Chavez, 2006, p. 142). Ultimately, this work calls for an intersection of place-based and border pedagogies, based on concepts of heteroglossia, meliorism, critical cosmopolitanism, nepantla, dialogic feminism, and pragmatic hope that form the basis of a new critical border dialogism.

Currere

According to Pinar (2011), curriculum should no longer reflect the static nature of a noun. On the contrary, the nature of curriculum should reflect the dynamism of its origin Latin action verb form, currere. Reframed as currere, curriculum becomes a "multiply referenced, conversation in which interlocutors are speaking not only among themselves, but to those not present, not only to historical figures and unnamed peoples and places they may be studying but to politicians and parents alive and dead, not to mention to the selves they have been, are in the process of becoming and someday may become" (Pinar, 2011, p. 43). As an ethical, political, and intellectual undertaking, the complicated conversation enables educational experiences, including teaching and learning (Pinar, 2011). This notion of currere has been under siege because of the current educational policies that connect curriculum to student performances on standardized tests. Educators have lost their intellectual and academic freedom to choose what they teach and how they will assess student learning (Pinar, 2011). As a consequence, students' and teachers' performances are measured according to the test score results of high-stakes, standardized assessments. In this manner, extremists have gained control of the U.S. school curriculum (p. 183). Critical border dialogism serves as a necessary component of all curricula, and furthers dynamic curricula, or currere (Pinar, 2011), by replacing all notions of static and complacency with rigorous, kinetic, and complicated conversation that engages us in problem-solving, including a grappling with the key issues of our time. Critical border dialogism, like currere, is also an intellectual endeavor (Carlson, 2005). The processes of critical border dialogism and currere are not mutually exclusive of one another, as both educational courses of action run the course of a complicated conversation.

Pinar (2011) laments the anti-intellectual conditions for teachers in public schools and for university education faculty alike. Anti-intellectualism is paradoxical as university faculty engaged in the study of curriculum issues, through the nature of their profession, must be engaged in intellectual pursuit (Carlson, 2005). Accordingly, many teacher education programs are currently preoccupied with quick prescriptions for teacher certification rather than subsumed with approaches such as a critical border dialogism as essential to the professional development of pre-service educators, classroom teachers, administrators, and other cultural workers. At this juncture, one could ask what role critical border dialogism might play in an uncharted future. First, before responding to this concern it must be noted that a critical border dialogism should make indispensable the contributions of educators and cultural workers as they address transnational and international issues, including their active engagement in promoting a sustainable abatement and end to ongoing wars, conflicts, and acts of terrorism. Second, in light of the present-day demands of our educational institutions and society, critical border dialogism serves as a worthy component of attempts to ameliorate current and ongoing issues while anticipating future points of conflict. Nelles puts forth the following positions: The national security concept has been so distorted, through preemptive or expansionist wars, militarism, and tolerance of human rights abuses, that a critical pedagogy approach must deconstruct its logical fallacies and misuses. It is especially important to assess the national security concept related to American domestic and foreign policy, including misuses of power (Nelles, 2003, p. 237). Nelles (2003) also pointed out that the United States has been waging its "war on terrorism" with no clear end and little respect for democracy, public opinion, persons, or even the sovereignty of other nations. Accordingly, the Iraq War set the stage for America's perpetual war based on a "unilateral global vision outlined in its September, 2002 National Security Strategy" (Nelles, 2003, p. 238). Given the realities of Nelles' predictions from over a decade ago, what role can critical border dialogism play in an eliminating the need for perpetual war and ongoing use of violence and intimidation in the pursuit of political aims? If history is any indication, there will certainly be new challenges to international stability and global efforts to maintain some sort of peace and order in regions of conflict. Critical border dialogism needs to engage stakeholders inside and outside of the academic community in taking on the issues of our time. There is a need for self-reflection and criticism on the part of other influential architects of public opinion, such as government, corporate, and media figures.

Educators, as cultural workers, have important roles to play in societal regenisis, or new beginnings. As Apple (2004) argues, educational institutions are not apart from society. Educational institutions are central "elements of that society—as workplaces, as sites of identity formation, as places that make particular knowledge and culture legitimate, as arenas of mobilization and learning of tactics, and so much more" (Apple, 2004, p. 158). Through a critical border dialogism, educators and cultural workers can examine, envision, and seek to broaden power relationships. By further contemplating the intersections of power relationships we, as a society, can begin to address issues of inequality and promote a socially just society.

TOWARD A CRITICAL BORDER PRAXIS

Educators, students, and cultural workers are empowered through the implementation of critical border dialogism as praxis. According to Freire (2005), praxis involves reflection and action to better transform the world. Therefore, praxis is a process through which theory and pedagogy are enacted; transformative objectives are conceptualized within the overarching goals of praxis in education. This definition of praxis follows Gramsci's (1971) recommendations for "commonsense" to be reformulated to turn common-sense ideas into informed knowledge. Informed knowledge, in turn, must be turned into the philosophy of praxis and applied across educational settings. Critical border dialogism with its concerns for heteroglossia, meliorism, critical cosmopolitanism, nepantla, dialogic feminism, pragmatic hope, pedagogy of place, and border pedagogy leads us down the path of a critical border praxis. Critical border praxis engages educators, students, and cultural workers in teaching and learning the social contexts of our discord and propels us to enter discourses and problem-solving that keep pace with our dynamic surroundings and allow us to move beyond our boundaries and perceived limitations. As Leonardo (2004) argues, there is a need for utopic thinking so that nightmares can be transformed into dreams. In this scenario we, as world citizens, enter a new epoch that will provide the narrative for a time of critical border praxis. Critical border praxis offers opportunities for educators, students, cultural workers, community leaders, and representatives of states and nations to come together for dialogue on the common goals for an era of security and relative peace. As part of critical border praxis education must reach out to those who had been deemed unreachable in the past. For critical border dialogism to be effective in its educational goals, anti-intellectualism should be replaced with access to first-rate, rigorous education. Contrary to the rhetoric that has been put forth by so-called education reformers, this sort of quality should not be hindered by the current push to drain public education from its resources. Support for public education stands in stark contrast to the increasing financial support and provisions for less-regulated charter schools or privately sponsored academies, which tend to divert already meager funding for public schools. On the contrary, all too often corporate or other non-public school interests further their agendas without sufficient state government oversight, thus reinforcing Bowles and Gintis' (1976) correspondence principle and Bourdieu's (1977) theories of cultural reproduction. There must be a shift toward first-rate public education for students regardless of their social-economic status. Quality education must be defined as something more than highly proficient standardized test scores.

Pax Americana and Pax Universalis

Critical border praxis is a concerted and mindful attempt to promote transnational understandings and models for change and peace. For critical border praxis to be efficacious, all efforts to promote meaningful, sustainable accord much reach beyond a Pax Americana, or period of relative peace for the United States, a concept that needs further scrutinizing and critiquing through critical border dialogism. Pax Americana has been put forth as being a bi-product of democratic peace theory. A key tenet of Pax Americana and democratic peace theory is that democracy in the United States has promulgated a period of improved relations with other democratic nations. Educators and their students should engage in a discourse of how democratic principles are positioned as a part of transnational and international conflict resolution. Rather than presuppose that the United States as a democracy adheres to conventions of a democratic peace, critical border dialogism should be a factor in determining how democratic principles influence peace (Brock et al., 2006). Accordingly, the United States and many of the world's current democratic institutions do not necessarily promote peace in the world. Rather, democratic governments "inculcate restraints in conflicts with other democracies" but the restraints can be circumvented by governments through covert warfare (Daase, 2006, p. 82). According to Daase (2006), there are incentives for democratic governments to use force for various reasons, such as diversionary action or in attempts to broaden domestic support through the expansion of war fervor. Moreover, peacetime provisions for "civil control of the military are lifted in times of war" (Daase, 2006, p. 82). Although there are attributes of democracy that make it a comparatively favorable form of government, peacefulness has not necessarily been a characteristic of democracies (Daase, 2006). In this manner, critical border praxis allows us critique the rhetoric associated with democratic notions of Pax Americana.

Critical border praxis is focused on movement toward a Pax Universalis, or universal peace, rather than a fixation on Pax Americana. Conflict resolution and genuine attempts to ameliorate societal problems are ongoing struggles and processes and further goals of a Pax Universalis. Critical border dialogism and critical border praxis provide for flexible starting places and follow-up courses of action for points of contention, as conflict resolution and struggle inherently engage us in Bakhtin's process of becoming.

Only when all parties involved, including nation-states, incorporate critical border dialogism into their educational curricula and international relationships will we see the possibilities for both short- and long-term solutions to misunderstandings, conflicts, and wars that cross international borders. It is these transnational understandings that offer the possibilities for addressing the root causes of long-standing international tensions and conflicts. The world needs well-educated and informed citizens who can contemplate and debate the potential and value of existing governmental systems, whether the policy makers in their governments represent functioning democracies, governments that are democratic in name only, or undemocratic governing bodies. Transborder dialogue has the potential to further understandings and offer possible conflict resolution for current conflicts at the time of concerns for a new Cold War, involving tensions between the United States, its NATO partners, and Russia. Beyond these looming hostilities, critical border dialogism provides pragmatic hope and a realistic path for the resolution of conflicts between Israel and Palestine, Nigeria and its internal strife, boundary disputes in East Asia, and innumerable conflicts and autonomy movements throughout the world.

Chapter 7

RECOMMENDATIONS

We, as members of societies, must transition from a culture of war to a culture of critical border dialogism and conflict resolution that continually promulgates shared visions and understandings. In our roles as educators, students, cultural workers, decision makers, and policy makers, we must transcend current culture wars through critical border praxis. Concerns and conflicts must be addressed through democratic participation. This engagement in democracy considers more than personal interests and individual agendas. Critical border praxis is informed by critical border dialogism and incorporates broader visions and worldviews than those that are limited to personal, group, or special interests. To explain further, critical border praxis should not be limited to concerns for single, one-dimensional issues. Moreover, hypocrisies within single-issue platforms should be exposed. For example, a person who participates in democracy based solely on their anti-abortion stances must also consider the hypocrisy of also being a death penalty supporter. To provide another case in point, if one seeks to further a personal agenda based solely on anti-capitalist stances, that same individual must be prepared to reflect on their own personal privilege.

Educational research can inform us of how critical border praxis is better facilitated. Accordingly, there is a need to consider the following questions:

1. How do current democracies, including the United States, incorporate understandings of the root causes of international conflicts in their larger visions of policy making?
2. How can nations prepare for the future by changing their present reactive stances to more proactive measures that promote long-term stability and reduce the likelihood of future violence and wars?
3. What role should education, in contrast to its traditional roles, play in developing rich understandings across physical, political, technological, ecological, and ideological spaces and borders?
4. How is critical border dialogism central to the development of a critical border praxis?
5. How does a critical border praxis serve as a genuine pre-emptive strike against inequality and social injustice?
6. How does the world overcome patriarchical, hierarchical systems, based on our understandings of dialogic feminism?
7. How does the United States as a nation, move from concerns for a Pax Americana to a vision for a Pax Universalis?

NEW BEGINNINGS

At local, state, or national levels critical border dialogism provides understandings of how to cross cultural, racial, ethnic, gender, sexual preference, religious, age, physical ability, and other boundaries. Unless highly focused attempts at dialogue are attempted, polarized gaps that ever-widen as the result of cultural, governmental, and military conflicts will continue to grow unabated. A requisite for a more civil society is that we stop shouting at each other and begin to listen. In this manner, democratic movements should be reassessed, but not abandoned. With regard to U.S. democracy, in particular, there must be serious reflection on the goals and future of our governmental system. In place of a government that is dominated by corporate and oligarchic interests, the U.S. system should move in the direction of respect for a multiplicity of voices as well as the socioeconomic and political interests represented by those voices. Likewise, critical border dialogism should allow opportunities for border crossings of national, racial, ethnic, religious, gender-restrictive, sexual identity, and ideological borders. It is long overdue that the United States, as a democracy, replaces gunboat diplomacy and drone-delivered terror attacks in the name of peace-making with genuine attention to the root causes of conflicts worldwide. It is time that the world revisits Mohandas K. Gandhi's observations of "an eye for an eye makes the world blind." We, as fellow beings, should not allow the efforts of Martin Luther King, Jr., Aung San Suu Kyi, Nelson Mandela, the Dalai Lama, Malala Yousafzai, and other indomitable individuals be in vain. Critical border dialogism, therefore, has a major role to play in providing answers to the above questions, or at the various least, addressing new sets of uncertainties as big questions are resolved. Furthermore, a critical border praxis engages the educational community in discourses that address issues facing our dynamic, fluid border environs. It is through a critical border praxis that we can begin to contemplate utopic ideals, no matter how unattainable those embodiments may seem. Critical border praxis provides conditions in which we, as educators and members of diverse communities of learners, are brought in from the margins to cross borders and broaden our possibilities to achieve what had been considered the unattainable. At local, state, and national levels resources need to be redirected toward educational efforts. This represents a shift in U.S. priorities from the current situation which pays homage to the 1950s by allocating a substantial share of the national budget to new forms of McCarthyism and a new Cold War. Under these conditions, overwhelming fear leads the United States into situations where national security hoaxes are commonplace. Place-based pedagogies, border pedagogy, and critical border dialogism are important for the development of a well-educated population and democratic society. As such, individuals should be afforded an education that promotes an understanding of their roles as local, national, and global citizens. Moreover, critical border dialogism engages educators, their students, and other cultural workers in the development of knowledges (Kincheloe, 2008) and subsequent understandings in classrooms and the larger society. Comparative, transnational currere and critical border praxis reinforce and help clarify the role of education, formal and informal, to influence individual thinking one-by-one, educate school-by-school, affect community-by-community, persuade policy makers state-by-state, and to transform country-by-country on the road to an enduring Pax Universalis.

Chapter 8

Transnational Educational Research in Four Countries*

Examples of Critical Border Praxis

INTRODUCTION

The research for this chapter was conducted in the following four countries: Malaysia, Mexico, Canada, and the United States. Throughout these investigations educators in each country reported on how they addressed U.S. policies in their respective curricula. Critical border praxis emerged as a theoretical construct as a result of these transnational studies. Critical border praxis provides a contemplation of the intersection of place-based and border pedagogies, as well as how pedagogies are central to understanding one's own situatedness. The findings of this study include recommendations for additional in-depth discussions of policies in the U.S. social studies curriculum. Implications for educators elsewhere are also articulated.

This cross-comparative study explores how U.S. transnational policies, including U.S. agreements and conflicts with other countries, have been taught in various settings. The research considers how to add breadth to the U.S. social studies curriculum through wider understandings of border pedagogy and place-based pedagogies. Included in this study are empirical analyses of data collected from educators and schools in Malaysia, Mexico, Canada, and the United States.

The first research took place in Sabah, Malaysia, with a study of Malaysian educators that transpired during and after a visit coinciding with the onset of the Iraq War. In Sabah, I witnessed the televised bombing of Baghdad and wondered how Malaysian educators would teach about the attacks launched on Iraq. Subsequent research in Chihuahua, Chihuahua, Mexico was undertaken before

---

* Content in this chapter was previously published as: Cashman, T. G. (2019). Transnational educational research in four countries: Promoting critical border praxis. *Journal of Research, Policy & Practice of Teachers & Teacher Education*, 9(1), 46–57.

drug cartel wars kicked into high gear in that country. A third study was conducted with educators in eastern Ontario, Canada secondary schools. Interviews, surveys, and focus group sessions were facilitated at three different school sites along the Canada and U.S. border. Finally, I carried out a case study of how U.S. educators teach transnational issues, including U.S. disputes and controversies, at a high school on the U.S. and Mexico border. The U.S. research provided a snapshot of how teachers addressed U.S. policies at that particular U.S. secondary school site.

Personal connections with issues can be the impetus for the development of research questions. I felt inextricably linked to global events during March 2003, while visiting future in-laws in Sabah, Malaysia. On March 20, 2003, at approximately 5:35 a.m. Baghdad time, U.S. bombs fell on Baghdad, Iraq. This initial attack was followed by days of severe bombing in Baghdad and other cities, coinciding with the invasion of U.S. and British ground forces in Iraq (Brunner, 2006). The unilateral actions were followed by huge protests in cities and towns across the United States and around the globe.

As a visitor to Malaysia, a Muslim-majority country, I was concerned as to how I would be received by local citizens, both Muslims and non-Muslims. Indeed, events during the onset of the war became a catalyst for gaining insight into how the U.S. invasion of Iraq and other momentous decisions of the U.S. government impacted lives of teachers and their students in Malaysia. I interviewed educators in Sabah, Malaysia, during June and July of 2003. Follow-up electronic communications with educators took place throughout the rest of 2003.

I made the decision to build on the study of teachers in Malaysia with comparisons of educators' perspectives in Mexico and Canada. Research for the study in Mexico transpired in Chihuahua, Chihuahua, a state that borders the United States. The Canadian sampling of teachers followed as research occurred in two eastern Ontario communities near the U.S. border. Finally, I sought to compare teaching approaches of U.S. social studies educators at a U.S. high school on the U.S. and Mexico international border.

It should be noted that research was completed in Malaysia and Mexico during the George H. W. Bush presidency; the data were collected in Canada and the United States during the first Obama administration. Guiding the research in all four cases was the desire to uncover comparative aspects of social studies educators who teach U.S. policies in their respective curricula. Accordingly, Phillips and Schweisfurth (2006) put forth, "To some extent everyone is a comparativist," and I set out to find the investigators in all of us, who seek to compare situations in familiar settings with environs less recognizable. Epstein (2008) argues that comparative education is an important endeavor because through comparative education we better comprehend and gain insight into the nature of our own education. Throughout the research in various settings educators reported on how classroom discussions ensued. My research sought to uncover the following: What perspectives do educators in

Sabah, Malaysia; Chihuahua, Mexico; eastern Ontario, Canada, and the U.S./ Mexico border bring to classroom discussions of U.S. policies, including recent U.S.-led wars and anti-terrorism measures? What do educators report as salient issues for students in their classroom discussions?

Research has indicated that there should be more candid, open dialogue on the effects of recent wars in U.S. classrooms (Flinders, 2005; Davis, 2005). According to Davis (2005), American students do not engage in discussions of recent wars as much as they should. Moreover, Davis maintains that "the school curriculum appears to be especially mute about this [the Iraq] war" (2005, p. 186). For the purposes of this study, I searched for perspectives that may have been lacking in the U.S. school curriculum.

Purpose of the Research

I chose to interview educators in Malaysia, Mexico, Canada, and the United States to better understand discourses with regard to U.S. policies in schools from three separate countries and compare their teaching with the case of a U.S. school site. I sought to provide additional comparative insight for those who educate on common issues in U.S. classrooms. In this study, I sought to address the following question: "How is the US curriculum enhanced through understandings of border pedagogy and transnational, comparative studies?"

This study provides perspectives on the impact of major U.S. policies, including the ongoing War on Terrorism. Indeed, some of these perspectives help fill the information void that has resulted from selective U.S. mainstream media censorship of war and terrorism perspectives.

Educators in all four settings were asked the following questions:

1. How much time is devoted to the discussion of U.S. policies?
2. How much open discourse exists in classrooms?
3. What, if any, ideological differences are evident in classrooms during their discussions that included U.S. policies?
4. How have discussions of U.S. policies changed over recent years?
5. Why are perspectives from other countries' social education classrooms important for U.S. social studies?

TRANSNATIONAL DIALOGUE

Gruenewald (2003) argues that a pedagogy of place promotes understandings of social and ecological places. By incorporating critical approaches into place-based pedagogies, "we challenge the assumptions, practices, and outcomes taken for granted in dominant culture and in conventional education" (Gruenewald, 2003, p. 3). Gruenewald's critical pedagogy of place, therefore, links pedagogy of place with critical theory. A critical pedagogy of place stands in contrast with the survival-of-the-fittest educational philosophy that currently prevails in much of the United States.

Border pedagogy builds upon critical understandings of place and attempts to connect those understandings with larger contexts. According to Giroux (2005), there are three components of border pedagogy that indicate respect for differences: (a) a recognition of margins, (b) the need for border crossers, and (c) a recognition of the historically and socially constructed strengths and limitations of places and borders. Borders are considered boundaries of entities, while the act of crossing borders involves going beyond existing boundaries and broadening one's perspectives of others in locales near or afar. Border pedagogy serves as a reconceptualization of existing ideologies and offers opportunities for students to engage the multiple references that constitute different cultural codes, experiences, and languages (Giroux, 2005). Border pedagogy provides possibilities for recognizing and contemplating historical contexts of our differences. As stakeholders in educational processes, teachers and students traverse languages, experiences, and voices and undergo changes in their own personal identities (Giroux, 2005).

The dynamics of what occurs in transnational classrooms can be considered through the lenses of border pedagogy. Giroux (1991) put forth that border pedagogy teaches students the skills of critical thinking, debating power, meaning, and identity. The goals of transformative education are embedded within the discourses of border pedagogy (Garza, 2007; Giroux, 1991; Romo & Chavez, 2006). According to Romo and Chavez (2006), border pedagogy encourages tolerance, ethical sophistication, and openness. Border pedagogy particularly engages learners in "multiple references that constitute different cultural codes, experiences, and languages to help them construct their own narratives and histories, and revise democracy through sociocultural negotiation" (p. 143).

Border pedagogy has implications for curricula in locales outside the border, itself. Comparisons, contrasts, and reflections on transnational education help provide multifaceted learning. Garza (2007) found that educators developed mutual understandings after considering border pedagogies. Moreover, teachers and administrators discovered that they could inform and strengthen each other's educational practices through transnational, border engagement (Garza, 2007).

Critical border dialogism (Cashman, 2015) considers the interconnectness of place-based and border pedagogies as part of contemplating one's own positionality in the context of larger research, intellectual knowledge, appreciation, and learning. Moreover, critical border dialogism is based on following principles:

- heteroglossia (Abraham, 2014; Bakhtin, 1981; Clark & Holquist, 1984) as it counters any sort of unilateral and unidirectional voices. Bakhtin (1981) puts forth that individuals connect with a multiplicity of voices through dialogue;
- meliorism (James, 1906; Koopman, 2006), which combines pluralism with humanism and serves as the thesis that we, as beings, are capable of bettering ourselves and creating a better world;
- critical cosmopolitanism (Delanty, 2006; Mignolo, 2000a), as it is an argument for the geopolitical diversal and globalization from below;
- nepantla (Abraham, 2014; Anzaldua, 1987; Maffie, 2007; Mignolo, 2000b), as it serves as a form of indigenous knowledge that places people and things in border surroundings that are characterized by dynamism and fluidity;
- dialogic feminism (Puigvert, 2012; Yaeger, 1991), as it is exemplified by creative energies with its renunciation, resistance, and counter-hegemonic actions of patriarchy and other borders that seek to limit
- pragmatic hope (Koopman, 2006; Nolan & Stitzlein, 2011; Shade, 2001), as it offers possibilities for a transcendence by our confrontation of the limitations currently imposed on our educational systems.

Reconstructionist approaches (Cashman, 2015) are needed for addressing the structural inequities in our present-day schools. Likewise, critical border dialogism offers hope for addressing the concerns articulated within the correspondence principle theory of Bowles and Gintis (1976). The findings of their research put forth the internal organization of schools corresponds to the internal organization of a capitalist society's workforce in its structures, norms, and values. In this manner, hierarchal control in schools reflects the structure of the market economy. Accordingly, diverse students of lower socioeconomic status have been systematically subjugated by the dominant class. Consequently, there is a pressing need for challenging power relationships with its theoretical underpinnings in heteroglossia, meliorism, critical cosmopolitanism, nepantla, dialogic feminism, and pragmatic hope.

Educators, students, and cultural workers are empowered through the implementation of critical border dialogism as praxis. According to Freire (2005), praxis involves reflection and action to better transform the world. Therefore, praxis is a process through which theory and pedagogy are enacted; transformative objectives are conceptualized within the overarching goals of praxis in education. This definition of praxis follows Gramsci's (1971) recommendations for "commonsense" to be reformulated to turn common-sense ideas into informed knowledge. Informed knowledge, in turn, must be turned into the philosophy of praxis and applied across educational settings. *Critical border praxis* engages educators, students, and cultural workers in teaching and learning the social contexts of our discord and propels us to enter discourses and problem-solving that keep pace with our dynamic surroundings and allow us to move beyond our boundaries and perceived limitations. As Leonardo (2004) argues, there is a need for utopic thinking so that nightmares can be transformed into dreams.

Method

For the research conducted in Sabah, Malaysia, interviews and surveys were conducted with teachers who taught students from ages fifteen to eighteen in either social studies courses at secondary and preparatory schools or General Knowledge, a required interdisciplinary national curriculum course at first year Malaysian higher education institutes. Permission was obtained so that personal interviews and follow-up communications could be conducted with nine educators, who represented Malay, Chinese, Iban, Sino-Kadazan, KadazanDusun, and Indian cultures.

In Chihuahua, Mexico, face-to-face interviews, focus group discussions, and observations were conducted with twenty-one social studies teachers and four school administrators at two separate sites, one secondary school and one middle school. For the Canadian comparative case study, ten secondary social studies teachers in three secondary schools in two eastern Ontario communities volunteered to be surveyed and interviewed. At the U.S. school site on the U.S. and Mexico border eight instructors and two administrators agreed to participate in the study. At least one teacher participant represented each social studies course taught at the high school. The participants self-identified as two females (one Latinx and one White) and eight males (five Latinx, two White, and one Black).

My research employed methodologies that followed Stake's (2000) model for a substantive case study. Accordingly, I reflected on impressions, data, records, and salient elements at the observed site, and outcomes of the study. Transcriptions were made of face-to-face interviews and focus group sessions with participants. The study also included logged written responses to survey questions. The researcher collected data and noted the frequency and categories of data. Interpretive explanations of observations, interviews, and archives followed (Creswell, 1998). The researcher served as participant-observer by interviewing participants and by collecting data from teacher responses to interview questions. Moreover, the author developed interpretive explanations of documents. For analysis of the overall case study, research took into consideration the recommendations of Yin (2003) for considering local meanings and foreshadowed meanings in their context. The work was reflective, with border pedagogy (Giroux, 1991) as a framework for uncovering contextual conditions relevant to phenomena (Yin, 2003).

A search for matching patterns followed Goodrick's (2014) guidelines for cross-case analysis. Goodrick states, "Pattern matching involves comparing two or more patterns between the cases to see if they are similar or different as a step in explaining observed processes or behaviors" (2014, p. 8). The resulting cross-comparative case study of U.S. policies, as taught in distinctively varied locales, produced comparisons and contrasts. Accordingly, the coding of data resulted in the following emergent themes:

1. Curriculum emphasis
2. Discussions of U.S. policies on war and terrorism
3. Comparative perspectives of government and society

DISCUSSION

Curriculum Emphasis

Although the amount of time devoted to discussions of U.S. policies in Malaysian classrooms was limited in the curriculum, such topics and issues were specifically addressed in a course entitled General Knowledge, a university preparation course. Other formal discussions took place as noted in course syllabi, but there was little time for extended discussion of U.S. policies outside of the specified school curriculum in government-supported schools.

On the other hand, the national curriculum in Mexico's publicly funded schools provided for the study of U.S. international relations in history and social studies courses at various levels. Overall, there was much interest in such discussions due to the intertwined U.S./Mexico relations, especially on the U.S. and Mexico border.

Canada's provinces have separate provincial curricula, so social studies and history education courses followed the Ontario curriculum in the sites studied. Canadian educators reported a high level of interest in the international affairs of the U.S. government, again, because of the interrelationships between the United States and Canada, both historically and ongoing. High levels of interest and engagement in discussion of U.S. policies were reported by the teachers at the Ontario school sites.

Educators at the U.S. school site on the U.S. and Mexico border, by contrast, increasingly followed a test-driven curriculum, as mandated by their U.S. state government. Discussions of the world-wide, transnational, national, and local effects of U.S. foreign policies were discouraged in lieu of an emphasis on lessons that put their state government and policies at the center of the curriculum. State assessments placed special emphasis on state history, government, geography, and economics. Although students demonstrated a high level of interest in U.S. and Mexico relations, in particular, there was very little time devoted to such discussions in the state curriculum. In effect, discussions of U.S. policies and issues were de-emphasized in favor of a testing system that placed an emphasis on state-driven agendas.

Discussions of U.S. Policies on War and Terrorism

Educators in Malaysia revealed students and classroom discussions centered around sympathy for the human casualties immediately after the September 11, 2001, attacks on U.S. targets. After the immediate post-9/11 period of compassion for their U.S. counterparts' losses, sentiments shifted toward hostility as the War in Iraq commenced. Classroom discussions of U.S. courses of action, including its war actions and justifications for its "War on Terror" reflected Prime Minister Mahatir's declaration of the United States being in violation of international laws. Educators reported that students believed that U.S. foreign policies were designed solely to favor U.S. interests, and the United States had its own definition of terrorism and terrorist activities.

Educators in Mexico shared that their students, too, were originally empathetic to the suffering of those in the United States who were affected by the 9/11 incursions. However, the tone of classroom discussions shifted dramatically after the bombings and ground invasion became full warfare in Iraq. Educators and their students discussed how the United States seemed to be embarking on wars without any sort of end in sight, and because of these policies their neighbor to the north, including large populations of Mexican background who were serving in the military or were simply U.S. residents, would be facing never-ending terrorism because of the U.S. government policies.

Canadian teachers also discussed how there was a shift in the tone of classroom discussions immediately post-9/11 and once the Iraq War began. There was almost unanimous opposition to the War in Iraq among the discussants, teachers, and students alike, over the U.S.-sponsored invasion of Iraq. On the contrary, Canada militarily supported the U.S. efforts in Afghanistan as necessary measures to prevent a complete takeover of the Afghan government by the Taliban or pro-Al Queda combatants. Public support for Canada's involvement in Afghanistan waned as Canada's own war losses in terms of human casualties increased.

The general consensus among the U.S. social studies educators was that there was a reluctance to discuss the U.S. wars in Iraq and Afghanistan in their classrooms. There were multiple reasons for this de-emphasizing of all recent U.S. international polices, and especially the ongoing wars. First, the state social studies curriculum puts greater emphasis on state and U.S.

domestic policies. In this manner, students were fully aware of the fact that the recent U.S. wars, campaigns on terrorism, and current U.S. international issues resulting from U.S. policies would not be addressed on their high-stakes examinations. Second, there may have been a reluctance on the part of the teachers themselves to explore the unfinished business of U.S. wars and campaigns on terrorism, due to their own lack of knowledge of intricacies and their personal choices to not engage in discussions that may be misinterpreted as overly sensitive or offensive to members of the school administration and local school district, parents, and students, themselves. Third, students rarely seemed willing to volunteer their attitudes and positions toward the current U.S. wars and efforts to curb terrorism from other seemingly remote parts of the world, unless the students had family members who were serving as active military and were stationed in countries such Iraq, Afghanistan, or other countries in military installations. Rather, students sought to pose questions of why drug cartel violence on the U.S. and Mexico border was not being addressed by the U.S. government as a form of terrorism. Educators noted the importance of being able to address the importance of such international issues that affected many of their students on a daily basis. At the same time, teachers and administrators offered that attention to such local, international issues and associations to wider global issues and contexts, receive short shrift in the social studies curriculum because of the high-stakes, test-driven nature of their courses. Students seek to engage in discussions of U.S. policies and issues, but they are afforded little opportunity for such involvement.

Comparative Perspectives of Government and Society

Overall, discussions of U.S. foreign policies in Malaysian classrooms moved toward concerns for their own nation's stability being threatened. The basic preoccupations were, as a Muslim-majority country, their inhabitants may have to face increased radicalism within their own country's borders while the United States continues to engage in warfare, under the auspices of the "War on Terrorism." Educators and students alike expressed the need to address the root causes of terrorism, rather than proceed with short-sighted policies that are designed to rally constituents around aggressions based on jingoistic declarations. In this manner, long-term solutions to conflicts have proved to be unattainable.

In the participating Mexican schools, educators reported that discussions moved away from seeing the United States as a model for resolving conflict with its policies. Educators, in fact, noted that some students argued that current problems in the United States were the result of the nation's past and current policies. To further clarify, students shared sentiments of the United States being in a position to reap what it has sown in terms of its past dealings with other countries, and in a sense expressed fatalistic views toward issues the United States must manage, including racial tensions, school violence, and wars with no clear end in sight. Some students believed that the United States, as a superpower, was crumbling from within and its citizens should pay heed to lessons of history and that the United States was, essentially, the "new Rome."

Interviewees and study participants in eastern Ontario, Canada, pointed out that comparative discussions of U.S. policies often revolved on differences and concerns over the major influences of the U.S. media and U.S. pop culture. As all of the Canadian school sites were situated in close proximity to the U.S. border, educators and students were in a position to frequently travel to U.S. locations, and make comparisons and contrasts with U.S. lifestyles and educational settings and the Canadian equivalents. As all of the participating Canadian communities had access to the U.S. media and pop cultures, there were concerns over the U.S. cultural influences and policies that directly affected their livelihoods and lifestyles. Classroom discussions also moved in the direction of how the United States and Canada had unresolved treaty issues that received little attention in the United States.

Students at the U.S. school site expressed their concerns for border drug cartel violence, and how ongoing criminal activity affected families on both sides of the U.S. and Mexico border, as many students either lived on the Mexican side of the U.S. border and crossed the international border to attend school at the U.S. school site, or they had relatives who lived in the nearby Mexican city and state. Educators reported that their students were eager to discuss how U.S. policies with Mexico and other countries, such as NAFTA, affected their daily lives. Because of state mandates that restricted the social studies curriculum, teachers and administrators at the U.S. school site maintained there was little time for in-depth discussions on such matters of interest to the students.

Of particular importance are the comparative discourses lacking in the U.S. case study. Accordingly, the following issues need further attention in the state curriculum:

- The legality of wars
- Treaty issues
- Immigration policies
- International perspectives of U.S. society and societal issues
- Crime, including white-collar corruption and violence
- Critiques of the mainstream media and pop culture
- The root causes of terrorism

THE URGENCY OF CRITICAL BORDER PRAXIS

In their ground-breaking study Bowles and Gintis (1976) argued that social conditions have been created by self-serving hierarchal, corporate, and military-industrial-congressional complex interests in our present-day educational institutions. Critical border dialogism offers the conviction that societal woes can, indeed, be addressed and ameliorated through quality educational experiences. Through this approach, we learn beyond our own political, geographic, historical, and philosophical borders. We must contemplate the multiplicity of voices, including the counter-hegemonic spaces of nepantla and dialogic feminism. Pragmatic hope offers a vision for the struggles that lay ahead for individuals and educational institutions that bridge local understandings with global interconnectedness. Educators and cultural workers need to engage in dialogue on the impact of cross-border conflicts on societies. There must be a deliberation on the economic, cultural, and political ramifications of transborder migrations and interactions. In terms of schools and the school curriculum, critical border dialogism and, ultimately, critical border praxis must engage professional educators and cultural workers in key roles of determining what is included or omitted from curricula. This stands in contrast to present conditions where lobbyists, textbook publishers, corporate sponsors, and policy makers are responsible for key decisions regarding curricula.

Critical border praxis, in particular, offers opportunities for educators, students, cultural workers, community leaders, and representatives of states and nations to come together for dialogue on the common goals for an era of security and relative peace. As part of critical border praxis education must reach out to those who had been considered unreachable in the past. Transnational educational exchanges previously deemed impossible must be held possible. For critical border praxis to be effective in its educational goals, anti-intellectualism should be replaced with access to first-rate, rigorous education. Contrary to the rhetoric that has been put forth by so-called education reformers, this sort of quality should not be hindered by the current push to drain public education from its resources. Support for public education stands in stark contrast to the increasing financial support and provisions for less-regulated charter schools or privately sponsored academies, which tend to divert already meager funding for public schools. On the contrary, all too often corporate or other non-public school interests further their agendas without sufficient state government oversight, thus reinforcing Bowles and Gintis' (1976) correspondence principle and Bourdieu's (1977) theories of cultural reproduction. There must be a shift toward first-rate public education for students regardless of their social-economic status. Quality education must be defined as something more than highly proficient standardized test scores. Critical border praxis is a concerted and mindful attempt to promote transnational understandings and models for change and peace. Critical border praxis incorporates broader visions and worldviews than those limited to personal, group, or special interests. Educational research can inform us of how critical border praxis is better facilitated.

Accordingly, there is a need to consider the following questions:

1. How can educational systems promote deeper understandings of the root causes of international conflicts?
2. How can educators teach of the benefits of proactive stances to promote long-term stability and reduce the likelihood of future violence and wars?
3. What role should education play in developing rich understandings across physical, political, technological, ecological, and ideological spaces and borders?
4. How can critical border praxis influence policy makers?
5. How does critical border praxis serve as pre-emptive action against inequality and social injustice?
6. How do we move toward a vision for a Pax Universalis, or a world truly reconstructed socially and politically based on mutual responsibilities, goals, and objectives?

Reconstructed Realities

A critical border praxis engages the educational community with discourses in issues facing our dynamic, fluid border environs. It is through a critical border praxis that we can begin to pursue utopic ideals, no matter how unattainable those embodiments may seem. Critical border praxis provides conditions in which we, as educators and members of diverse communities of learners, are brought in from the margins to cross borders and broaden our possibilities to achieve what had been considered the unattainable. At local, state, and national levels resources need to be redirected toward educational efforts. Comparative, transnational critical border praxis reinforces and helps clarify the role of education, formal and informal, to influence individual thinking one-by-one, educate school-by-school, affect community-by-community, persuade policy makers state-by-state, and to transform country-by-country on the road to an enduring Pax Universalis.

CONCLUSION

The findings of this study support what Nelles (2003) noted after the September 11, 2001, attacks:

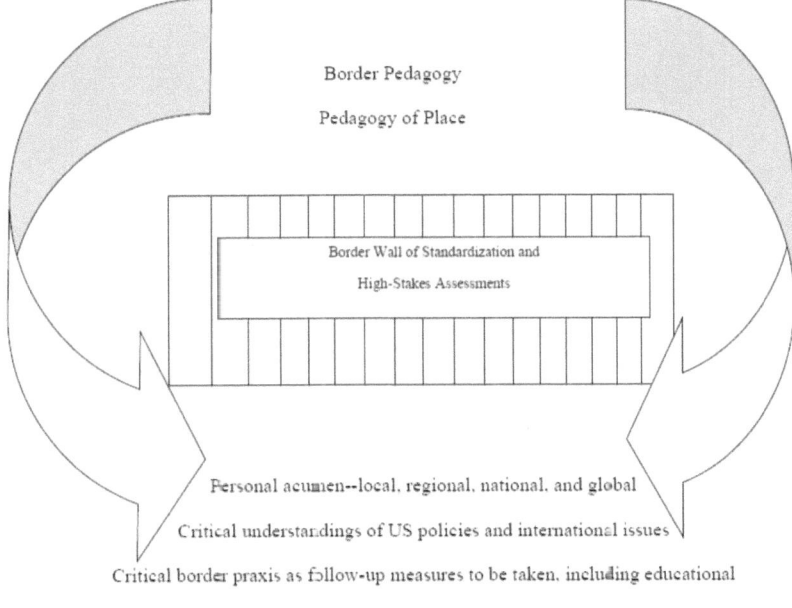

Figure 8.1 Components of Critical Border Praxis.

Ironically, within days of 9/11, outpourings of sympathy came from around the world, some even saying, "We are all Americans now." Within a year the United States had squandered most international goodwill and generated unprecedented anti-American sentiments from millions of people in scores of countries. (p. 238)

Thus, if genuine change is to occur, the present U.S. educational system must play a significant role in investigating and addressing the root causes of global conflicts (Cashman, 2013). Through the varied lenses of border pedagogy educators should look critically at policies that separate us and begin to understand what Hampton et al. (2003) describe as the "wedges that educational and power systems push between children and quality educational experiences." Border pedagogy serves as a useful framework for transnational comparisons of curricula, and a subsequent broadened understanding of what curricula should embody (see figure 8.1).

Chapter 9

"In Spite of the Way the World Is"*

What U.S. Educators Can Learn from Their Counterparts in Cuba

INTRODUCTION

The following chapter provides another example of the pressing need for transborder dialogue, transnational educational discourses, and critical border praxis. The case study took place in Cuba during an educational exchange to Cuban secondary and university educational sites. Cuban educators of pedagogy and social education engaged in dialogue and shared information on how they address U.S. policies during their classroom discussions. The research provides comparative perspectives on how educators address issues affecting two countries with a history of governmental tensions. The investigation examines how teachers in Cuban classrooms engage in discourses on the recent developments in Cuban and U.S. relations, including the teaching of historical and territorial issues. This research considers border pedagogy, critical border dialogism, and critical border praxis as approaches for those who educate on the effects of U.S. policies. Ultimately, pragmatic hope offers the possibilities for an emergent third space for Cuba and U.S. relations, including educational exchanges.

The research was conducted toward the end of the second Obama presidential administration in the United States at a time when commercial flights were commencing between the United States and Cuba. Since the research was conducted, however, the opportunities for dialogue among Cuban and educators are now closing due to recent decrees issued by the U.S. national government. As of June 4, 2019, the Trump administration imposed new restrictions on Americans going to Cuba. The United States will not permit

---

* Content in this chapter was previously published as: Cashman, T. G. (2019). "In spite of the way the world is": What United States educators can learn from their counterparts in Cuba. *International Journal of Comparative Education and Development*, 22 (1), 16-29. https://doi.org/10.1108/IJCED-11-2018-0050.

group educational and cultural trips known as "people to people" trips to the island the Treasury Department announced. In effect, the U.S. Department of the Treasury seeks to discourage and intimidate would-be educational researchers with additional layers of bureaucratic procedures.

The new mandates run contrary to what many in the field of education have advocated; namely, better cooperation among professionals in both nations. Research has argued for shared knowledge, particularly in the field of social studies, through a critical border dialogism (Cashman, 2015) and ultimately, critical border praxis (Cashman, 2016a), as necessary approaches for transnational education, cooperation, and conflict resolution across transnational borders.

Interviews and surveys took place with Cuban professors of pedagogy and social educators to discern how they address U.S. transnational policies in Cuban classrooms. The research provides comparative perspectives of how Cuban educators engage in discourses of Cuban relations with the United States, given a recent history of governmental tensions. The research presented in this paper, in turn, seeks to promote mutual understandings of one's own society and local, state, and national educational systems. This work also promotes reflection on how educators in Cuban classrooms promote a contemplation of recent developments, including the teaching of historical and territorial issues. This research, in turn, seeks to provide additional insight for those who promote transnational understandings and whose responsibilities include teaching on the effects of U.S. transnational policies.

The investigator observed and identified historical and cultural differences evident in Cuban classrooms. This study ultimately considers the possibilities for third spaces and common grounds between the U.S. and Cuban educational systems. Bhabha (1994) developed the concept of third space as a metaphor for the space in which cultures meet. Thus, the following paper calls for a "trialectical" approach that challenges binary, dualistic assumptions of educational understandings of the Cuban educational system (Lefebvre, 1991). According to Soja (2009), trialectical thinking challenges all conventional modes of thought and postulated epistemologies. The following question guided research: "How can U.S. educators learn from the perspectives of their peers in the Cuban educational system?"

EDUCATION IN CUBA

Educators perform their responsibilities under unique conditions influenced by that country's historical background, sociocultural conditions, and government policies. These circumstances influence the present-day curriculum, and, in some cases, place constraints on the discourses that take place in classrooms. In Cuba, education is the social institution that follows the Jose Martí's notion of "To educate is to free."

Since the 1960s, the Cuban government has sought to raise the quality of Cuban education for students from rural and working-class urban backgrounds (Carnoy et al., 2007). Government policy fixed incomes so that there was little variation among the salaries of workers and professionals. Education "quickly became a highly desirable profession" (Carnoy et al., 2007, p. 29).

All future educators attend government-run pedagogical institutes so that a well-designed national curriculum is taught. The ministry of education sought to send well-prepared teachers to every school in Cuba, including remote, rural schools in distant provinces (Carnoy et al., 2007). This situation has changed due to the rapidly growing tourist industry. As tourists pay in U.S. dollars, and a parallel dollar economy has developed. According to Carnoy et al. (2007),

> A chambermaid in a hotel, for example, may earn $30-$50 in tips per month (or more), double or triple the teacher's salary. Competition from tourist industry jobs has drawn off highly skilled labor from teaching, creating shortages in the teaching force. (p. 32)

Cuban elementary students outperform their peers in other Latin American countries on math and language tests. Cuban children attend schools intensely focused on instruction and staffed by well-prepared, regularly supervised teachers in a social environment that is dedicated to high academic achievement for all social groups. Combining high-quality teaching with high academic expectations and a tightly controlled school management hierarchy with well-defined goals augment the results the Cuban system produces. It distinguishes Cuban education from other systems in Latin America. The Cuban system gives most Cuban pupils a primary education that only upper-middle-class children receive in other Latin American countries (Carnoy et al., 2007, p. 141).

Lutjens (2007) argues that we can learn lessons about social theory, critique, and praxis in educational settings by analyzing Cuba's experiences. There is a need for more scholarship on Cuban educational policy and schooling practices. Moreover, the level of interest in Cuban education has dramatically increased.

THEORETICAL FRAMEWORK

Paolo Freire visited Cuba to observe the successes of that country's literacy campaign, and Freire's experiences in Cuba influenced his overall perspectives. In effect, Cuban literacy workers undertook a "concientization" process (Freire, 2005) and sought to awaken the minds of their students to the oppression that had pervaded their lives, through their teachings. In Cuba, the pedagogical approaches were much more explicit with regard to political topics; Freire favored a slower, discovery approach to the selection of active, generative themes (Kozol, 1978). Working-class learners in Brazil eventually generated topics very similar to those set forth in Cuba, the process of learning was of paramount importance to Freire. In Cuba, the urgency of the revolution and the economic and military threats posed by the United States engendered a more direct and politically charged approach to the problem of illiteracy (Supko, 1998, p. 12).

A necessary condition for further understandings of the Cuban educational system is a sense of place. Gruenewald (2003) argues for a pedagogy of place, at it serves as a means of examining the connections between individuals and their inhabited spaces. For the purposes of this study, place-based pedagogies promoted understandings of social and ecological places. Critical approaches integrated into place-based pedagogies "challenge the assumptions, practices, and outcomes taken for granted in dominant culture and in conventional education" (Gruenewald, 2003, p. 3).

Border pedagogy, in turn, builds upon critical understandings of place in the Cuban context and attempts to connect those understandings with larger contexts. According to Giroux (2005), border pedagogy involves a recognition and understanding of margins as affected by history, power, and difference. Moreover, an individual must contemplate historically and socially constructed limitations to become a border crosser who has developed new understandings of others (Giroux, 2005). Borders become boundaries of entities, while the act of crossing borders entails going beyond existing boundaries and broadening one's perspectives of others in locales near or afar. Cervantes-Soon and Carrillo (2016) put forth "a border pedagogy is possible on a grand scale in which (not only) the critical, but also the spiritual, emotional, and the marginal come together to rearticulate education for social transformation" (p. 299). This approach recognizes the "articulations of border thinking among students living at the margins and within the liminal spaces of collision between the Third and First Worlds" described by (Anzaldúa, 1987).

In the case of Cuba and the United States, political and historical issues have served as roadblocks to border crossings post-Cuban revolution. Critical border dialogism (Cashman, 2015) provides approaches for building bridges between Cuban and U.S. educational communities. The recommended dialogic conversations draw upon a critical pedagogy of place and border pedagogy and integrate the following principles: heteroglossia, meliorism, critical cosmopolitanism, nepantla, dialogic feminism, and pragmatic hope.

For the purposes of this study, research seeks to bridge the lack of communication and subsequent understandings of how similar issues are addressed by educators in the United States and Cuba, countries with a history of cross-border tensions. The knowledge gained from comparative studies of the Cuban educational system and other empirical case studies can be part of efforts to alleviate larger governmental and cross-societal tensions. Critical border dialogism is a starting point and draws upon a critical pedagogy of place and border pedagogy while incorporating the following principles:

- heteroglossia, (Abraham, 2014; Bakhtin, 1981; Clark & Holquist, 1984) as it counters any sort of unilateral and unidirectional voices. Bakhtin (1981) puts forth that individuals connect with a multiplicity of voices through dialogue;
- meliorism (James, 1906; Koopman, 2006), which combines pluralism with humanism and serves as the thesis that we, as beings, are capable of bettering ourselves and creating a better world;
- critical cosmopolitanism (Delanty, 2006; Mignolo, 2000a), as it is an argument for the geopolitical diversal and globalization from below;
- nepantla (Abraham, 2014; Anzaldúa, 1987; Grande, 2004; Maffie, 2007; Mignolo, 2000b), as it serves as a form of indigenous knowledge that places people and things in border surroundings that are characterized by dynamism and fluidity;
- dialogic feminism (Puigvert, 2012; Yaeger, 1991), as it is exemplified by creative energies with its renunciation, resistance, and counter-hegemonic actions of patriarchy and other borders that seek to limit;
- pragmatic hope (Koopman, 2006; Nolan & Stitzlein, 2011; Shade, 2001), as it offers possibilities for a transcendence by our confrontation of the limitations currently imposed on our educational systems (see table 9.1).

Heteroglossia, meliorism, critical cosmopolitanism, nepantla, dialogic feminism, and pragmatic hope were components of the data analysis. Heteroglossia was an essential consideration throughout the study as multiple interpretations of Cuban and U.S. historical, political, economic, societal, cultural, and geographic interconnectedness emerged. Meliorism factored into Cuban educators' commitments to their professions and revealed an appreciation for pluralism and humanism among the participants. Those who agreed to be involved with this research demonstrated a belief in the notion that they were creating better selves, students, and members of society regardless of their lack of government funding; and, in particular, the dearth of access to broadband internet technologies due to the continuing U.S. boycott of Cuba. Critical cosmopolitanism developed as a major component of this study as educators put forth different

Table 9.1 Components of Critical Border Dialogism and Critical Border Praxis

Heteroglossia	Meliorism	Critical Cosmopolitanism	Nepantla	Dialogic Feminism	Pragmatic Hope
Considerations for multiple meanings	The human condition can be improved	Cosmopolitan, worldly assumptions are challenged	Indigenous knowledge plays a central role	Critiques of patriarchy	Prospects for legitimate advancement
Dialogism is a key characteristic	Pluralism and humanism are joined together	Border thinking is a necessary epistemology	"Survivances" in the face of colonization	Voices are engendered and consider intersections of feminist practices and dialogic voices.	Teachers collaborate to resolve issues in schools
Positivist social science and linguistics are disputed and resisted	An alternative to both pessimism and optimism	A medium of societal transformation based on the principle of world interconnectedness	A belief system that places people and things within a colonized borderland	Members are empowered to overcome patriarchy and its inherent violence	The current system of punishment-and-rewards is challenged; third spaces emerge

→ Critical border dialogism
→ Critical border praxis

conceptualizations of human rights and democracy as recommended by Mignolo (2000a). Mignolo (2000a) argues for challenges to a world order governed by global capitalism and new forms of coloniality. Mignolo recommends a bottom-up approach to cosmopolitanism, as opposed to a traditional top-down hierarchy. Nepantla emerged as a key aspect for this study as colonized perspectives in the Cuban education system were replaced by more indigenous and self-determined viewpoints post-Revolution. In this manner, "survivances" (Grande, 2004) provided new perspectives within post-colonial Cuba. Dialogic feminism was preeminent in that patriarchy emerged as an enduring refrain in Cuban society, despite a new awareness of gender roles and gender violence. Finally, pragmatic hope offers possibilities for a transnational community of inquiry, where U.S. and Cuban educators collaborate to resolve issues in schools. Pragmatic hope offers the prospects for an emergent third space, an inclusive area of opportunities for mutual and individual revelations.

According to Freire, praxis involves reflection and action to better transform the world. Therefore praxis is a process through which theory and pedagogy are enacted; transformative objectives are conceptualized within the overarching goals of praxis in education. Critical border praxis engages educators, students, and cultural workers in teaching and learning the social contexts of our discord and propels us to enter discourses and problem-solving that allow us to move beyond our boundaries and perceived limitations.

In the case of Cuba and the United States, negotiated third spaces are possible. According to Bhabha's (2004) concept of third space, effective discourses and subsequent encounters offer the prospects of producing something new and substantially different, or a third space. Bhabha's (2004) third space theory puts forth that cultures are constantly in a process of hybridity. This hybridity relocates histories and sets up new configurations of authority and political proposals. The process of cultural hybridity produces something distinctive and new interventions among meanings and interpretations. The third space is a mode of articulation, a way of describing a productive, and not merely reflective, space that promotes new possibilities (Meredith, 1998). It is a space of new forms of cultural meaning and production blurring the limitations of existing boundaries and calling into question established categorizations of culture and identity (Bhabha, 2004). According to Bhabha, this hybrid third space is an ambivalent site where cultural meaning and representation have no unifying concepts or fixed in space (Bhabha, 2004). Soja expands on Bhabha's constructs and takes issue with some interpretations of hybridity. Accordingly, "Third space is a space where issues of race, class, and gender can be addressed simultaneously without privileging one over the other; where one can be Marxist and post-Marxist, materialist and idealist, structuralist and humanist, disciplined and transdisciplinary at the same time"

(Soja, 2009). In essence, this third space transpires after pragmatic hope has come to fruition.

QUESTIONS GUIDING RESEARCH

This study focused on how Cuban educators taught, discussed, and addressed U.S. transnational policies in classrooms. Cuban professors of pedagogy were asked to respond to a common set of face-to-face interview question, and structured observations were made at the various Cuban school sites. Overall, research focused on how Cuban educators taught, discussed, and addressed U.S. transnational policies in classrooms. The following questions guided research:

1. How much time is devoted to the discussion of U.S. policies in Cuban classrooms?
2. How much open discourse exists in classrooms?
3. What, if any, cultural and ideological differences are evident in classrooms during their discussions that included U.S. policies?
4. How have discussions of U.S. policies changed over recent years?
5. Why should others, and particularly Americans, be informed of perspectives in Cuba's social studies classrooms?

METHOD

As part of an educational exchange between U.S. and Cuban universities, U.S. educators applied for a program co-sponsored by the Pedagogical University Enrique José Varona, the University of Havana and participating U.S. universities. U.S. participants visited cultural sites, engaged in official functions, and presented workshops at the participating universities, a Havana university preparatory school, a rural public middle school, a Havana elementary school, government pre-school, cultural centers, and an annual literacy conference. For the purposes of this study, the researcher interviewed and surveyed educators who taught university students in pedagogy. Ten professors of pedagogy participated by responding to open-ended questions. Another Cuban professor assisted in the bilingual interviews, providing translations whenever needed and serving to clarify communications, whether verbal or nonverbal. Informal interviews and translations were conducted with school administrators and teachers. Observations took place in middle school, preparatory high school, and university school sites and classrooms. Data were collected from personal observations, photographs, video recordings, and audio recordings.

The researcher employed methodologies that followed Stake's (2000) model for a substantive case study. Impressions, data, records, and salient elements at the observed site were recorded. Transcriptions were documented for face-to-face interviews and hour-long focus group sessions. Participants also logged responses to written survey questions. Data collection included notations on the frequency and categories of data. Interpretive explanations of observations, interviews, and archives followed (Creswell, 2013). The researcher developed interpretive explanations of documents. The subsequent data analysis explicated themes and patterned regularities (Creswell, 2013). For the overall case study, there was a consideration for the recommendations of Yin (2003) for examining local connotations and foreshadowed meanings in their contexts. Border pedagogy (Giroux, 2005) served as a framework for uncovering contextual conditions relevant to phenomena (Yin, 2003).

Data analysis followed what Glesne (2011) refers to as thematic analysis, whereby the data were read many times in search of emerging themes or categories and subcategories. This also corresponds with Creswell's (2013) description of a data analysis spiral, wherein the analysis process is iterative, including multiple coding phases. Initial data analysis began during the interviews themselves (Glesne. 2011). Themes emerged during the interviews and follow-up questions were formulated to elicit more information on the emergent themes. The coded data was organized into major themes or categories. After member checking with participants, counterexamples of major themes were considered to ensure the interpretations were trustworthy.

Coding captured the data related to the initial interview questions. The major themes that emerged from coding were as follows:

1) curriculum emphasis,
2) discussions of U.S. transnational policies,
3) comparative perspectives of government and society, and
4) self-reflections on Cuban education.

Follow-up electronic communications with the Cuban participants verified the interpretations put forth by the researcher. The most obvious limitation to this study is, as a case study, the limited scope of perception.

FINDINGS

Research consisted of interviews, focus group sessions, and observations conducted with Cuban university professors of pedagogy at school sites in and around Havana, Cuba. Transcriptions and notations provided the researcher with categories of data. The following sections elaborate on the four main emergent categories: (1) curriculum emphasis, (2) discussion of U.S. transnational policies, (3) comparative perspectives of government and society, and (4) self-reflections on Cuban education. The accounts of participants from their one-on-one interviews, focus group sessions, and classroom visits are reported under the aforementioned headings.

Curriculum Emphasis

Most participants (8 out of 10) pointed to Jose Martí as the father of Cuban comparative education and an advocate of educational reform in the Latin American context. Martí articulated the need for foundations of Cuban curriculum and contextualized assessment. Thus, assessment in the U.S. context was not necessarily appropriate for Cuban schools. Post-revolution curriculum revision entails a consideration for pedagogy as science, critical pedagogy, and human development. The Pedagogical University Enrique José Varona has led the way for curricular change and augmentation.

Educators reported the Cuban model of pedagogy includes a responsibility to promote scientific pedagogical approaches. In this manner, participants considered the curriculum a strength and attribute of the Cuban education system. Comparative education researchers such as Jose de la Luz y Caballero and Felipe Perez Cruz have recorded and analyzed developments in the Cuban education system that have distinguished it from others worldwide. In particular, this curricular thrust has sought to "rescue" Cuban education and the Cuban school curriculum from colonial perspectives and colonized thinking. For example, the principles of *Cubation* dictate there is no room for segregation based on race in Cuban schools. Moreover, teamwork and collaboration are essential expectations for educators and students alike. A common goal among all educators is the intellectual, psychological, physical development, and well-being of the whole child.

Participants noted that quality education is a priority in Cuban society. Accordingly, teachers receive one day off per week for curriculum implementation and professional development. Action research is an integral part of all teachers' responsibilities. Discussions of the interrelationships and common, overlapping histories of Cuba and the United States are part of the Cuban school curriculum. Included are numerous points of contact between Cuba and the United States, including current events, the U.S. War with Spain when Cuban revolutionaries took control of Santiago. Educators reported that students study Americans such as Henry Reeve, an individual who fought for the Cuban cause. Other classroom discussions center on how Jose Marti lived in the United States for a time period and, conversely, on how Americans such as Ernest Hemingway resided in Cuba. Participants also addressed other intersections of Cuban and U.S. relations with less frequency.

Educators noted there is an allowance of 10 minutes every day for a discussion of current world events at all levels of education. In this manner, students are engaged in almost daily dialogue on Cuban and U.S. relationships. The content of discourses is determined and organized according to the specific needs of each grade level. One participant noted that discussions of the United States in the curriculum are a "part of everyday life" for Cuban students. Cuban educators, a part of focus group sessions, put forth it is "normal to discuss problems between the United States and Cuba in the curriculum" and the United States is included in the Cuban school curriculum at all levels.

Discussions of U.S. Transnational Policies

Cuban educators reported there are discussions of the strong U.S. influences on Cuban history and important points of contact between Cuba and the United States. Prominent figures addressed in the Cuban school curriculum are Abraham Lincoln, Malcolm X, and Martin Luther King, Jr. The root causes of important U.S. events, such as the U.S. Civil War are part of classroom deliberations.

Interviewees put forth their students understood the importance of the U.S. decision to not allow Cuban rebels to keep control of Santiago during the U.S. War with Spain. Cubans successfully fought and captured that city only to see it handed to the United States. As a result, leaders of the Cuban revolt, including Jose Martí, openly expressed their embitterment with the lack of support from the United States. Resentment still exists today over the treatment of Cuba during that time period. Students discuss how the U.S. government perceived Cuba as a weak and incapable of self-determination, and, consequently, an entity ripe for exploitation. Cuban educators discuss recent and current tensions between Cuba and the United States on an almost daily basis. A more recent example of the lack of communication and trust between Cuba and the United States is the rejection of the Cuban government's offer for support, including medical expertise, after Hurricane Katrina.

In summation, individuals and focus group participants noted a strong emphasis on Cuba and U.S. relations in their courses. They put forth their discussions, for the most part, and focus on resolving differences and finding hope for future Cuba and U.S. relationships, in spite of disagreements between the governments of the two nations. Even though concepts of patriotism in Cuba and the U.S. differ, Cuban educators recommended an examination of common spaces between Cuba and the United States.

Comparative Perspectives of Government and Society

Cuban educators reported discussing the numerous contradictions found within the U.S. society. One participant noted that in spite of the U.S. trade embargo, Cuban society is "bombarded" with U.S. popular culture, including mainstream films. However, Cuban citizens who received permission to visit the United States and traveled to the United States found that the U.S. films viewed in Cuba do not accurately reflect U.S. realities. In essence, the common person in the U.S. lives in contrast to the portrayals of wealthy U.S. citizens portrayed in popular, mainstream films. Cuban educators recommended a more realistic portrayal of marginalized people by the U.S. media.

Study participants reported they found U.S. individuals to be open and approachable, which contrasts with the official U.S. government positions of alienation from Cuban residents. Participants also noted Cubans identify with the common citizens of the United States. They were aware of support for better U.S./Cuban relations from large segments of the U.S. population. Cuban educators cited the need for further, more extensive collaborative research among Cuban and U.S. scholars.

When asked what the U.S. education system can learn from Cuban education, the most common refrain was that U.S. teachers should realize Cuban individuals seek closer relations with the people of the United States. Study participants noted that both governments, Cuba and the United States, have adopted dissimilar restrictive policies for their citizens. These established policies severely restrict educational interchanges. Accordingly, they maintained that more intensive, ongoing exchanges among Cuban and U.S. educators are requisite for the promotion of deeper appreciations of each other. Most notably, there needs to be an examination of common values and values that differ. Discussions of why there are shared values and juxtaposed values must ensue. As one participant put forth during the focus group sessions for this research, "Competition is part of the root causes of terrorism." Indeed, accusations of terrorism are rife between Cuba and the United States and conversely.

Doctora Lidia Turner Martí, Professor Emeritus at Enrique Jose Varona University of Pedagogical Sciences, proffered, "We (as Cuban educators) work for a better world, in spite of the way the world is." This pedagogical approach is, indeed, applicable to educators in both countries.

Self-Reflections on Cuban Education

Cuban educators were willing to self-critique their own educational system and note both the successes and tasks facing their current educational institutions. Study participants noted that ongoing, dynamic reconstruction is a challenge facing their education system, just as it is in other educational systems throughout the world. An attribute of the Cuban educational system is its willingness to draw on comparative educational research to make adjustments suited to the Cuban education. Educators recommended continued prioritization and investment in education by the government.

Educators also proposed further collaboration among society's professionals with teachers and local schools. They expressed a need for common language among pedagogues and other professionals. Moreover, study participants argued for a continued emphasis on professional development for Cuban society. Accordingly, the quality of teachers has a profound effect on the education of future leaders in Cuba.

Study participants noted their desires for the following enhancements to their education system:

(1) more interdisciplinary learning within the Cuban educational system,
(2) a continued emphasis on critical pedagogy, and
(3) access to technology that keeps pace with a new generation of digital environments and an information society.

Educators argued for continued spaces and allowances for self-reflection. They offered there should be critiques on the roles and portrayals of women in Cuba. Participants, both female and male, reported that Cuban patriarchy is perpetuated in corners of society in spite of recent changes in attitudes.

Educators noted there is a governmental will to promote equality among LGBTQ, but the Cuban government is discovering there is a struggle to change long-standing beliefs. Sexual orientation is discussed in schools, but discrimination still exists in the larger society. Participants maintained attitudinal change is taking place "little by little."

Other challenges to the Cuban education system include finding an appropriate balance between academic and vocational education. According to Cuban educators in this study, more than 90 percent of youth aspire to attend a Cuban university. Yet, societal needs call for more students pursuing some sort of vocational education.

DISCUSSION

Cuban educators noted it was important for educators in the United States and Cuba to conduct educational exchanges and communications as current and historical problems are a part of discussions in Cuban classrooms. The proximity of Cuba to the United States allows for tensions that are part of the everyday lives of most educators and their students alike. At the same time, Cuba and the United States share a common history. From the hopes of Cubans for positive relations with the United States during the Cuban revolution against Spanish rule, when colonial Cuba played the role of a key site for the transport of supplies to modern disagreements, including the U.S. trade embargo and treaty issues, there have always been important contacts between Cuba and the United States. U.S. historical figures such Abraham Lincoln and Martin Luther King, Jr., are deemed role models for Cuban students.

Earlier studies (Cashman & McDermott, 2013; Cervantes-Soon & Carrillo, 2016; Glenn, 2007) argue for the potential of empowered students in border settings to critically consider issues and envision their roles as global citizens. Effective dialogue between the United States and Cuba is a pre-requisite for the development of these educational insights. Ultimately, concerted and meaningful discourses put into place a framework for critical border praxis. Critical border praxis consists of concerted and mindful efforts to promote transnational understandings and models for change and peace (Cashman, 2016a).

Critical border praxis, therefore, plays an important role in addressing new sets of uncertainties. In this manner, questions of how the United States as a nation can move from concerns for a Pax Americana, a period of relative peace within the U.S. domestic borders, to a vision for Pax Universalis, or period of universal peace. Furthermore, educational communities should be engaged in discourses on the issues facing dynamic, fluid border environs. It is through a critical border praxis that we can begin to contemplate utopic ideals, no matter how unattainable those embodiments may seem. There is a pressing need for educators and members of diverse communities of learners to cross borders and broaden possibilities to achieve what is considered the unattainable. In Cuba and the U.S. resources need to be prioritized and redirected toward education on national, state, and local levels. In the case of both countries, a substantial share of the budget remains invested in military spending. By prioritizing educational development both Cuban and U.S. educators can strengthen our educational systems. Education, formal and informal, is then allowed to transform perceptions one-by-one, school-by-school, community-by-community, and to influence policy makers state-by-state, and to reconstruct education country-by-country on the road to an enduring Pax Universalis. Ultimately, this Pax Universalis will serve as a third space where students and educators alike are positioned as co-creators of knowledge and agents of change.

Cuban educators put forth educational exchanges and communications among Cuban and U.S. educators serve to provide additional understandings to classroom discussions of current and historical problems between the two countries. The proximity of Cuba to the United States allows for tensions that are part of the everyday lives of most educators and their students alike. At the same time, Cuba and the United States share a common history. From the hopes of Cubans for positive relations with the United States during the Cuban revolution against Spanish rule, when colonial Cuba played the role of a key site for the transport of supplies to modern disagreements, including

"In Spite of the Way the World Is"   101

Table 9.2 Critical Border Praxis and Lessons Learned from Cuban Educators

Heteroglossia	Meliorism	Critical Cosmopolitanism	Nepantla	Dialogic Feminism	Pragmatic Hope
Cuban educators share how U.S. figures are addressed within the elementary and secondary curriculum	Cuba sustains the highest literacy rate in Latin America	Grass roots movements have played an integral role in the Cuban literacy movement	Indigenous Cuban culture, including a strong focus on Cuban arts, plays a central role	Educators put forth "progress" has been made, but systems of patriarchy need to be changed further	Cuban educators expressed hope for future educational exchanges of knowledge, practices, and technologies
As individuals, Cuban educators are required to reflect on and self-critique their personal pedagogies	Cuban education provides for a pluralistic society	Cross-border studies are part of professional development at Enrique Jose Varona University of Pedagogical Sciences	Cuba has maintained a consciousness for its own self-determination, despite extreme U.S. pressures	Women at the highest levels—school administrators, university presidents, and government officials are voicing their concerns	Horizontal, vertical, and transnational dialogue among Cuban educators and international colleagues must be continue, and in the case of the United States, be enhanced
Cuban university professors offer critiques of their own university systems	Cuba serves as a net exporter of medical doctors to the rest of the world	Cuban educators express their hopes for more transnational exchanges, especially with U.S. colleagues	Cuban has resisted attempts at further colonization	Discussions of how to empower and overcome patriarchy are taking place at various educational and governmental levels	An emergent third space offers the possibilities for effective dialogue and educational praxis

the U.S. trade embargo and treaty issues, there have always been important contacts between Cuba and the United States. U.S. historical figures such Abraham Lincoln and Martin Luther King, Jr., are recognized as role models for Cuban students (See Table 9.2).

Implications

If future relations between Cuban and the United States are deemed uncertain, critical border praxis has an essential role in addressing new sets of uncertainties. This study recommends that educational communities engage in discourses addressing ongoing issues facing our dynamic, fluid border environs. Critical border praxis provides conditions in which we, as educators and members of diverse communities of learners, become cross borders and broaden our possibilities to achieve what had been considered the unattainable. Resources need to be prioritized and redirected toward educational efforts on national, state, and local levels so critical border praxis becomes a reality. Both societies, Cuba and the United States, should make even larger investments in their educational systems. Through transnational and transborder engagements, such as educational exchanges, both U.S. and Cuban educators are provided opportunities to reflect on the strengths and weaknesses of their own educational systems. The role of education, formal and informal, then serves to transform perceptions one-by-one, school-by-school, community-by-community, and to influence policy makers to reconstruct education country-by-country as part of pragmatic hope for an enduring Pax Universalis. Pax Universalis serves as a third space where transborder students and educators alike are positioned as co-creators of knowledge and agents of change.

This research highlights the necessity for zones of mutual respect and cooperation among educators as part of a new, emergent third space intersecting Cuba and the U.S. educational communities. Collective memories of traumas and tensions experienced cannot, and should not, necessarily be erased from the histories of Cuba and the United States as common educational understandings are the key starting point for a critical border praxis. Critical border praxis implements ongoing dialogue between the two countries and offers pragmatic hope for the futures of both nations and opportunities to ameliorate relationships between neighbors with over sixty years of hostilities. This emergent third space is possible through sustained critical border praxis, a praxis that seeks to address the unaddressed points of contention and bridges that need crossing between the countries. In this manner, educators from the United States, Cuba, and other settings work for a better world, in spite of the way the world is.

Chapter 10

"They Did Not Make Their Decisions on a Whim"

Teaching Border Issues on the United States and Mexico Border

INTRODUCTION/CONTEXT OF THE STUDY

While previous chapters considered the importance of transborder understandings and educational exchanges in locations such as Malaysia, Mexico, Canada, Mexico, and Cuba, chapter 10 refocuses attention to the education of students on the U.S. side of its border with Mexico. This most recent study set out to uncover whether or not tenets of critical border praxis were a part of teaching and learning in sixth grade classrooms. Recent dramatic shifts in educational policies and local issues, such as the COVID-19 pandemic concerns still remain imminent, and, in some cases, replace other pressing issues.

As the world's attention has been focused on the all-too-often lethal COVID-19 virus, uncertainty has become the "new normal" for educational systems, from pre-school through higher education. Prior concerns, including the issues surrounding immigration and the mistreatment of refugees, including children, are placed on the back burner. However, if anything the need for resistance to government policies that include the imprisonment of youthful migrants and a "Stay in Mexico" policy that places young and old migrants' lives in eminent or immediate danger. For the purposes of this study, the researcher set out to uncover what sorts of current, relevant social studies issues were being addressed in upper elementary classrooms on the U.S. and Mexico border.

Background

The issues surrounding immigration and the mistreatment of refugees, including children, have often been overlooked in elementary social studies classrooms. However, there is a need to challenge and re-think government policies, including the imprisonment of youthful migrants and the Trump administration's "Remain in Mexico" policy that places young and old migrants' lives in eminent or immediate danger (Rosenberg, 2020). This study seeks to uncover how current, relevant social studies issues were being addressed, or not being addressed, in upper elementary classrooms on the U.S. and Mexico border. The concerns and pedagogical approaches implemented by educators in two schools from the same school district are examined. The socioeconomics of the student populations reflected the overall demographics of the border communities serves. Thus, one of the elementary school sites was listed as qualifying for 100 percent of their student population under the guidelines for federal funding of free and reduced lunches, whereas the second elementary site was receiving federal funding for 70 percent of their students within the Free and Reduced National School Lunch Program (New Mexico Public Education Department, 2018).

The U.S. and Mexico Border

Martínez (1994) and Staudt and Spener (1998) argue that borders are spaces where diverse and contradictory elements converge. A border does not simply divide two countries. "Instead, the border region should be viewed as an energetic, constantly changing area where new possibilities are always on the horizon" (Flores & Clark, 2002, p. 9). Fuentes and Peña (2010) identified the U.S./Mexico border as a location of multiple transnational urban communities that are highly productive in terms of the global economy. Martínez (1994) defined the U.S./Mexico border as an interdependent borderlands region, whereby border regions in both countries are symbiotically linked. In this case, the symbiotic link is economic. Currently, issues related to Central American migration across the U.S. and Mexico border, particularly from the Northern Triangle countries, predominates official U.S. government policies and mainstream media discourses.

Border Pedagogy

For the purposes of this study, the dynamics of what occurs in social studies and interdisciplinary language arts and social studies classrooms are considered through the lenses of border pedagogy (Cashman & McDermott, 2013; Flores & Clark, 2002; Garza, 2007; Giroux, 1991; Reyes & Garza, 2005; Romo & Chavez, 2006). Giroux (1991) stated that border pedagogy draws upon diverse cultural resources that promote new identities within existing configurations of power. Border pedagogy is facilitated to promote within students the skills of critical thinking and debate as well as to develop their own self-identities. Additionally, students build greater senses of place, both locally and globally. In the context of this study, border pedagogy is put forward as a means of providing students with better contemplation and clarification of their positions within a region, state, nation, and worldwide. Embedded within the discourses of border pedagogy are the goals of transformative education (Garza, 2007; Giroux, 1991; Romo & Chavez, 2006). Romo and Chavez (2006) offer that border pedagogy encourages tolerance, ethical sophistication, and openness. Thus, border pedagogy works to decolonize and revitalize learning and teaching to promote liberty and justice for all. Border pedagogy particularly engages K-12 students in multiple references that constitute different cultural codes, experiences, and languages to help them construct their own narratives and histories, and revise democracy through sociocultural negotiation.

The goals of border pedagogy coincide with the educational goals of promoting literate, critical, and independent learners (Reyes & Garza, 2005). As educators strive to meet the needs of English language learners on the U.S./Mexico border, who have distinctive family traditions and cultural identities, their work has implications for social studies education outside of geopolitical border regions (Cashman & McDermott, 2013).

With the increase of immigrant and refugee populations in U.S. communities, the role of border pedagogy has expanded to non-border communities (Ramirez et al., 2016). Border pedagogy is not a recipe for the success of Latinx students in education. Rather, it is a way to disrupt the manner in which marginalized youth are educated (Reza-Lopez et al., 2014). Border pedagogy can serve to broaden the understandings of teachers and students to foster critical thinking, learning, inclusion, and activism to improve conditions inside and outside classrooms.

RESEARCH METHODOLOGY

This study follows on Stake's model of a substantive case study for examining naturalistic phenomena. Transcriptions for the oral responses to questions in face-to-face interviews were recorded. Data collection included notations on the frequency and categories of data. Interpretive explanations of observations, interviews, and archives were compiled (Creswell, 2013).

The study focused on educators and multiple perspectives from school administrators and those who teach sixth grade social studies and interdisciplinary language arts. Questions posed to educators on included the following:

1. How do you feel about the amount of time devoted to social studies in elementary classrooms? How might this affects students later?
2. How do you feel discussions of border issues in social studies classrooms can impact students?
3. How much time is available for discussion of border issues and U.S. transnational policies? How can these ideas be age appropriate?
4. What types of discussions of current events take place in your classroom, including discourses on the issues surrounding Central American migration?
5. How might controversial issues be better addressed in classrooms?

Data analysis followed what Glesne (2011) refers to as thematic analysis, whereby the data were read many times in search of emerging themes or categories and subcategories. Research also implemented Creswell's (2013) recommendations for a data analysis spiral, wherein the analysis process was iterative, including multiple coding phases. Initial data analysis began during the interviews (Glesne, 2011). The coded data from interviews and follow-up questions were categorized into emergent themes.

Three sixth grade teachers, two administrators, and one elementary student provided input, including reflections, observations, and personal perspectives for this study. The participants represented two separate school sites from the same school district positioned on the U.S. side of U.S. and Mexico international border. In terms of gender and ethnic/racial and ethnic background one teacher identified as Latinx of Cuban family background, and the other two teachers identified as Latinx of Mexican-American heritage. The two administrators self-identified as Latinx and African American. The elementary student identified as Asian American. In all, three males and three females provided contributions. Thus, research participants represented racial, gender, and ethnic backgrounds consistent with the demographics of a school district positioned in the United States in close proximity to the U.S. border with Mexico (see table 10.1).

Data coding, pattern identification, and theme articulation were essential to the post-data analysis of video- and audio-recorded interviews and observations. Accordingly, codification and categorization produced the following emergent themes:

1. Time/emphasis concerns;
2. Local concerns/considerations;
3. Pedagogical approaches/reflective practice;
4. Professional development concerns;
5. Other specific considerations, including recent immigration;

Table 10.1 Traits of Participants

Name	Position/ Years of Experience	Gender	Racial/Ethnic background	School Site
Mr. A.	Grade 6 Social Studies/ Mathematics teacher (41)	Male	Latinx (Mexican-American	Border Elementary
Mr. B.	School principal (40)	Male	African American	Border Elementary
Ms. C.	School principal (21)	Female	Latinx (Mexican-American)	Southwest Elementary
Mr. D.	Grade 6 Language Arts/ Social Studies teacher (15)	Male	Latinx (Mexican-American)	Border Elementary
Ms. E.	Grade 6 Social Studies/ Language Arts teacher (15)	Female	Latinx (Cuban-American)	Southwest Elementary

DISCUSSION

The following major themes emerged from observations and interviews with administrators and teachers on the U.S. and Mexico border and their use of border pedagogy: (1) time/emphasis concerns; (2) considerations for local issues; (3) pedagogical approaches/reflective practice; (4) the need for additional professional development; and (5) discourses on recent immigration.

Time/Emphasis Concerns

At the two participating school sites educators, including all administrators and teachers, recommended the provision of more instructional time for social studies teaching and learning. Accordingly, the local school district needed to emphasize interdisciplinary social studies in the school curriculum prior to Grade 6. This change is currently viewed as oppositional to the local school district's current focus on improving language arts and mathematics state assessment test results. Two teachers, in particular, maintained that by strengthening the social studies curriculum test scores in language arts and mathematics are not adversely affected, and students' cognitive performances actually improve. As such, they provided specific, necessary approaches for teaching social studies content and provided evidence of making social studies an essential component of interdisciplinary pedagogical approaches. Moreover, the two administrators expressed the need for more in-depth approaches to social studies content in classroom instruction.

Sixth grade social studies teachers at two school sites maintain the current emphasis on language arts and mathematics leaves students lacking in their knowledge of social studies concepts by the time students reach their last year in the school district's K-6 elementary schools. For example, the following benchmarks are part of the state standards that are based on the Common Core State Standards Initiative for sixth grade social studies (Common Core State Standards Initiative, 2020):

> Border Elementary teacher Mr. A noted, "Social studies and science alternate days so they only receive 45 minutes of social studies every other day; it meets 3 times one week and 2 times the next. It has a huge impact on how much social studies knowledge students have." The sixth grade social studies state curriculum follows the Common Core State Standards curriculum. Under Content Standard 1, 5-8 Benchmark 1-A, 6.1 students are expected to describe the relationships among ancient civilizations of the world. Furthermore, under Content Standard 1, 5-8 Benchmarks 1-C, 6.1: 1-C, 6.4: and 1-C, 6.5 students are to describe and compare the characteristics of the ancient civilizations and explain the importance of their contributions to later civilizations; describe major religions of the world to include Hinduism, Buddhism, Judaism, Christianity and Islam; and compare and contrast the geographic, political, economic, and social characteristics of ancient civilizations and their enduring impacts on later civilizations.

According to Mr. A, overall interest and knowledge of ancient and world civilizations, are impacted by the lack of emphases on social studies concepts in grades kindergarten through five. Mr. A. recommends providing additional supplemental readings and classroom resources to better facilitate social studies teaching and learning in early elementary and intermediate level (Grades 3–5) classrooms. Mr. A. reported that the school district purchased one set of social studies textbooks for his sixth grade classroom during the past school year. He noted the textbooks proved to be useful for supplemental readings and classroom resources, yet additional educational resources are needed for effective teaching and learning of the Common Core Social Studies State Standards.

Mr. D. has been an educator for fifteen years. He noted that social studies classes do not meet daily so, Mr. D., as their language arts and social studies teacher, compensates for this shortcoming by incorporating historical fiction for his class assignments. He reflects on his teaching by noting, "In my class we try to fit in discussions of issues whenever we can. I search for materials of interest that are age appropriate." Mr. D., even though he is assigned to teach both language arts and social studies courses asserted, "We are bound ethically to teach history, in spite of the time constraints. When we teach social studies issues, we teach empathy." He argues teaching empathy should be an essential part of the curriculum given all of the violence and trauma that surrounds our students. Moreover, the current educational system needs to focus upon the importance of compassion. Mr. D. further stresses the need for student engagement when he stated,

> Nobody remembers the handout on reptiles, but they remember those big discussions on colonization, culture, and economic situations. We need to have those deep-seated conversations. It's not happening anymore.

Mr. D. described how he specifically focused on the following Common Core Social Studies State Standards: Content Standard 1,5-8 Benchmark 2-E, 6.1, explain how human migration impacts places, societies and civilizations; Content Standard 1, 5-8 Benchmark 2-E, 6.2, describe, locate, and compare different settlement patterns throughout the world; and Content Standard 1, 5-8 Benchmark 2-E, 6.3, explain how cultures create a cultural landscape, locally and throughout the world, and how these landscapes change over time. With regard to current immigration and refugee issues, he seeks to draw correlations with other historical events, such as the Holocaust during World War II.

Sixth grade social studies and language arts teacher at Southwest Elementary, Ms. E., reveals her students lack the necessary background in social studies education. She asserts her students should possess knowledge from all of the social studies disciplines by Grade 6. Throughout her fifteen years of teaching social studies she has observed more of an emphasis on the rote memorization of social studies concepts. Nonetheless, Ms. E. makes it a point to focus on the following Common Core Social Studies State Standards: Content Standard 1, 5-8 Benchmark 1-D, 6.1, organize information by sequencing, categorizing, identifying cause-and-effect relationships, comparing and contrasting, finding the main idea, summarizing, making generalizations and predictions, drawing inferences and conclusions; Content Standard 1, 5-8 Benchmark 1-D.6.2, identify different points of view about an issue or topic; and Content Standard 1, 5-8 Benchmark 1-D.6.3, use a decision-making process to identify a situation that requires a solution; gather information, identify options, predict consequences, and take action to implement that solution.

Her contention is the following: "I don't want students to lose the *fun* of social studies." Ms. E. impresses upon her students the relevance of social studies in their everyday lives. Accordingly, if students are not provided with opportunities to learn social studies, "We are doomed to keep making the same mistakes." She also stresses to her students, "If you cannot make informed decisions, others will make decisions for you."

The principal at Border Elementary School, Mr. B, observed that Grade 6 is an extremely important transition year. He put forth,

> Prior to Grade 6 social studies is blended with language arts instruction. By Grade 4 teachers should be using an integrative approach for social studies in their classrooms. However, as the instruction ends up being test-driven, language arts skills often take priority in classrooms. The curriculum should be more comprehensive.

Mr. B. noted, on a positive note, that among his staff some teachers take extra measures to address social studies concepts lacking in the school curriculum. For instance, one teacher supplements classroom learning by taking students on an educational travel trip each summer. The local school district, however, does not provide funding for this or other field trips. This situation occurs in a school district that is ranked as "high-poverty" with more than 75 percent of the students eligible for Free or Reduced Priced Lunch (FRLP) under the National School Lunch Program (New Mexico Public Education Department, 2018).

Mr. B., as an administrator, lamented the lack of district-funded field experiences to better augment the social studies curriculum. Although educational class trips were once commonplace within the school district, most of the school-sponsored field experiences have been eliminated in recent years. Mr. B. observed there have been budget cuts that have eliminated educational trips once considered and experienced by students and their teachers as a school tradition.

The principal at Southwest Elementary School, Ms. C., put forward there are numerous flaws with districtwide social studies education and argued there has been a de-emphasis of social studies concepts in most elementary school classrooms. As a result, she argued the following:

> Students are not as prepared for high school social studies. We need vertical and horizontal alignment for social studies education. Students are not tested until 8th grade, so social studies content is not emphasized earlier.

She also put forth the need for ongoing professional development in social studies pedagogy and reasoned, "Teachers need a stronger background in the social studies to teach it well." She sensed the potential for efficacious pedagogy among her faculty, yet offered, "Only two of my teachers fully integrate social studies with their language arts instruction. Those two teachers do an excellent job." The principal contended students must wait until the eighth-grade social studies curriculum to engage in content designed to prepare students for the statewide social studies standardized examination. Accordingly, she felt students were not receiving the necessary social studies background knowledge and were being set "up for failure when they get to high school and beyond."

Considerations for Local Issues

At Southwest Elementary, Ms. E. reported that her students share bi-national, bilingual, and bicultural identities and are deeply affected by immigration rhetoric and policies. She offered the following:

> My students are concerned over the closure of borders, as they cannot visit relatives. They bring those concerns to my classes. They cannot return to Mexico, and their families in Mexico cannot visit them.

The two school sites for this study are both located within walking distance of the U.S. and Mexico border. Consequently, both administrators, Mr. B. and Ms. C., noted interactions among cross-border migrants and U.S. Border Patrol agents on school property. The two principals also expressed concerns for the security and safety of their students.

According to Mr. B., "Immigration has always been part of the picture here locally." However, more recently attention, including classroom discussions in some instances, has been afforded to the concerns of refugees and migrants from Central America, Cuba, Brazil, and Africa seeking to cross local borders into the United States. However, Mr. B. stated discussions of immigration issues, including Central American immigration, is not observable in most classes.

As principal of Southwest Elementary School, Ms. C. revealed that there has been limited discussion of cultural diversity at her school site, with the exception of holiday celebrations throughout the year. Her goals, past and present, include presiding over an educational setting that values diversity and emphasizes mutual respect. As the administrator of a school site in the same school district as Mr. B., she also laments the cutbacks in funding for educational field trips. Ms. C. maintains additional funding is needed for the facilitation of learning outside of traditional classroom settings and for the provision of experiential, community-based learning.

Pedagogical Approaches/Reflective Practice

At Border Elementary Mr. A. noted there is a lack of instructional materials for social studies in kindergarten through fifth grade. Prior to Grade 6 all social studies instruction is to be incorporated into a language arts block. The curriculum is test-driven in all grades, but all teachers focus on improving test scores for language arts and mathematics.

Mr. D. reported that he incorporates the teaching of local, national, and international issues as a part of daily language arts lessons. He purposefully combines the teaching and learning of social studies concepts and border issues together with literacy skills. Mr. D. also observed an improvement in standardized language arts assessments through the teaching of interdisciplinary social studies concepts in his language arts courses.

In Ms. E.'s classroom at Southwest Elementary students engage in project-based learning during their social studies classrooms. The personal responsibilities of students include investigating the biographies of influential individuals in world cultures such as Malala Yousafai, and subsequently composing opinion papers. Ms. E. stated that she also facilitates active learning projects for ancient civilizations as specified within the Common Core Social Studies State Standards. Ms. E. noted these approaches have become an integral part of border pedagogy for her students. For their ancient civilization projects students select and research an ancient civilization. Next, the students compile and share with their peers an interactive notebook based on what they learned. Students attach sticky notes and literary analyses, as well as opinion papers and research papers within their interactive notebooks. As a consideration for the large number of immigrants in her classroom she recounted "For my English language learners I use social studies cognates to assist them."

Mr. B., Border Elementary principal, highlighted the effectiveness of one language arts and social studies teacher at his school site. He put forth this individual was particularly efficacious in the teaching and learning current events, including immigration and border wall issues. As a part of classroom pedagogies, that particular teacher asks his students essential questions and uses student-generated questions for discussions on local issues. Part of his border classroom pedagogy is to share a famous quote each week with his students. Students are asked to interpret and discuss the implications of the passage. The quote, in turn, becomes the theme for all coursework that week.

Mr. B., in his role as an administrator, also noted pressures to receive high test scores in language arts and math were driving pedagogy and the curriculum. As such, he recommended that social studies teaching and learning "needs to be more comprehensive." He pointed out the successes of teachers who effectively integrate social studies with language arts, elicit student-generated questions in their teaching, use a famous quote to frame the curriculum and instruction for each week, and sponsor summer trips and extension activities. Mr. B. observed, "The possibilities for effective social studies are there." He indicated so by pointing out the following:

> Some teachers promote learning about immigration by having students read youth novels such as *Esperanza Rising* and *House on Mango Street*. In such

cases students are learning social studies concepts and developing social studies knowledge in their language arts classes. One language arts teacher has sought to compare and contrast the treatment of Jews with the present policies toward Central American refugees. Students read *Boy in the Striped Pajamas* which is set during the Jewish Holocaust and follows up with a compare/contrast of the current treatment of refugees and immigrants.

Southwest Elementary School principal, Ms. C., maintained there are only two teachers on her staff that fully integrate social studies content and standards with their language arts instruction. She is currently promoting a further integration of social studies in early elementary and intermediate level grades. Ms. C. offered that social studies holds the potential to reinforce the K-6 curriculum throughout.

The Need for Additional Professional Development

Educators offered several recommendations for ongoing professional development of efficacious social studies education at their school sites. First of all, they stressed the need for more reflective practice among the faculty members. Second, educators at the two school sites noted the need for teachers with stronger backgrounds and expertise in social studies education. For example, they contended that most teachers do not have pedagogical understandings of how to teach and promote understandings of controversial issues. They also argued that professional development for social studies education should be ongoing, as teachers must be prepared to constantly revise and incorporate new social issues as a part of their teaching and learning. Educators suggested many teachers lack the necessary academic and pedagogical knowledge to effectively teach the varied and dynamic aspects of social studies.

According to the participants, interdisciplinary approaches, including social studies concepts, must be developed. To accomplish these goals there must be an allowance for and an incorporation of reflective practices. In terms of recommendations from individual educators, Mr. D. put forth that all teachers need to be well read and informed on current issues. He also maintained, "We are bound ethically to teach history," in spite of time constraints in the curriculum. According to Mr. D., if we assist our students in the contemplation of essential questions, we become more effective change agents.

At Southwest Elementary Ms. E. recommended that her fellow educators become more knowledgeable in the various social studies disciplines. Hence, the main components of social studies including geography, government, sociology, anthropology, psychology, and economics, as well as history, should all be addressed in interdisciplinary courses. In particular, there is a need for critical discourses within integrated social studies and language arts courses.

The two school administrators also provided recommendations for social studies teacher education. Mr. B. put forth that newer preservice educators and recent university education program graduates "seem more attuned to interdisciplinary approaches" for teaching social studies. He also stated there is a need for both internal and external funding for learning outside the four walls of classrooms, and professional development should allow for teachers and students alike to learn through educational field experiences.

Ms. C., Southwest Elementary principal, stated that teachers need stronger content knowledge, teacher preparation, and professional development for social studies teaching and learning. Observations of efficacious classroom teaching and learning have provided her with insight into what precipitates better student performances. She perceived students better engage with all subject content readings when social studies connections are included as a part of classroom pedagogies.

Discourses on Recent Immigration

At Border Elementary both Mr. A. and Mr. D. shared how they facilitate discourses on local issues and recent immigration patterns, Mr. A. reported he wanted students to "do their own thinking and come up with their own conclusions." Mr. D. put forth he feels social studies issues must be effectively integrated with language arts instruction. To accomplish these goals he addresses Core Curriculum Social Studies State Standards by teaching with historical fiction and film.

Ms. E., Southwest Elementary teacher, noted her personal family connections with refugee and immigration concerns. As a Cuban immigrant whose family left her native country during the Cuban Revolution, her family moved to Spain and then immigrated and put down roots in the southwestern United States. She stated the following:

> More and more we're hearing about undocumented migrants from Central America. I try to make connections with within the curriculum, including when we're talking about ancient Greece, or whatever unit we're on. I connect it with current issues. Some of these people are escaping horrific conditions, and they did not make their decisions on a whim, just like my family did not make the decision to leave Cuba on a whim.

At Border Elementary School the school principal, Mr. B., offered the following perspectives: "Here locally we have people who are passing through our campus on foot that are either refugees or people who are seeking to be US residents." Yet, he recounted that he rarely observes teacher-led discussions on the ramifications of recent immigration, including the more recent increase in those who seek refugee status from Central America, Cuba, Brazil, other Latin American countries, and Africa. According to Mr. B., the location of the school on the U.S. and Mexico border translates to immigration issues as a daily reality for the educational community. However, there is currently a little open discussion on how most immigrants are seeking economic opportunity and new conditions to improve their overall existence and standard of living. Mr. B. added,

> My concerns as a school side principal are for the safety of my students and my staff. I don't hear discussions about of most recent immigration including Central Immigration Central American immigration in most classes. The older students are perhaps most impacted and they are willing to discuss. On the other hand, I do have one teacher who poses questions to his students about what would you do if you lived in Honduras or Guatemala right now and you are facing violence and extortion.

Ms. C., Southwest Elementary School principal, recommended more discourses on immigration issues as a part of language arts readings. She stated, "Students can definitely relate to those readings." Ms. C. also offered concerns for how refugees from Central American may impact future student registration and enrollment in the local school district.

Overall, educators in this study put forth the followingrecommendations for more effective elementary social studies pedagogy and reflective practice:

1) The necessity of more instructional time for social studies;
2) a conscious and deliberate integration of more social studies content and concepts as part of interdisciplinary teaching and learning;
3) less superficial representation of cultures, including Central American, within classroom discussions;
4) an avoidance of the heroes, holidays, and favorite foods approaches;
5) more active teaching and learning approaches, including project-based learning for students;
6) emphasizing better professional preparation in social studies pedagogy for preservice teachers;
7) requiring current teachers to engage in professional development and workshops for the overall improvement of social studies education;
8) and, modeling and incorporating pedagogical approaches that promote empathy and compassion.

A Student's Perspectives

A former sixth grade student at Border Elementary, Student G., provided personal recommendations for the teaching of social studies in elementary school classrooms. She reflected on her experiences with coursework at her elementary school. Student G. reported,

> Before sixth grade, I don't really remember much of what I learned in social studies. We did read about the Middle Ages, the feudal system, and the history of knights. But there was very little class discussion. In comparison, in sixth grade I remember learning how Germany went into debt after WWI, leading to a depression. This led to Adolf Hitler gaining followers and power. By gaining power, Hitler was able to overthrow the German government. He then started controlling Germany and later Poland. I remember this because we read a lot of books and watched films that supported the books. We read the books *War Horse* and *The Boy in the Striped Pajamas*. Our class also watched the movie *The Pianist*. We visited the local Holocaust Museum. We discussed everything we learned in class and compared it to what is happening in our world today. We described how Jewish, disabled, and other people who didn't fit into Hitler's idea of "pure people" were being killed and the United States didn't do very much to aid them. As a class, we compared this to what is happening with refugees and immigrants today. The US has the ability to help immigrants and give them a better life, but we are pushing them away and sending them back to usually unsafe living. conditions. After comparing the situations and talking about it, we discussed how we should avoid making the same mistakes Germany did.

The testimonial provided by Student G. serves to reinforce the idea of how interdisciplinary social studies content can address Content Standard 1, 5-8 Benchmark 1-D, 6.1, organize information by sequencing, categorizing, identifying cause-and-effect relationships, comparing and contrasting, finding the main idea, summarizing, making generalizations and predictions, drawing inferences and conclusions; Content Standard 1, 5-8 Benchmark 1-D.6.2, identify different points of view about an issue or topic; and Content Standard 1, 5-8 Benchmark 1-D.6.3, use a decision-making process to identify a situation that requires a solution; gather information, identify options, predict consequences and take action to implement that solution.

DISCUSSION

As evidenced by Student G.'s reflections and recollections, border pedagogy and interdisciplinary social studies teaching and learning serve as key factors in student retention of social studies knowledge. In essence, a pondering of the essential questions, supported by readings, film recordings, and outside the classroom experiences that supported student engagement in learning and committing to memory social studies concepts.

Previous research (Cashman & McDermott, 2013; Shear et al., 2018; Smets, 2019; Ward, 2018) concurs with the recommendations put forth from educators in the two U.S. schools located within close proximity to the U.S. and Mexico border. Earlier studies have recommended more instructional time for social studies, effective integration of social studies concepts, in-depth explorations of culture, engaging social studies pedagogies, better professional preparation and ongoing professional development for social studies education, and incorporating significant social studies issues in teaching and learning.

Students engage in controversial immigration issues such as amnesty policies and border policing when provided a non-judgmental and safe environment in social studies classrooms. Inquiries emerge from contentious issues, and those open-ended essential questions allow for the discussion of controversial subject matter. Smets (2019) puts forth the importance of educating teachers and children on how to provide a welcoming and inclusive environment for immigrant and refugee students. Smets notes,

> Teachers and schools also need our support to make sure teachers enjoy adequate training, and we ensure that psycho-social and language learning support is provided where needed, and we need to involve parents in the school community. (2019, pp. 314–315)

New American Economy (2019) provides data to assist teachers and their students discuss the impact of immigration and refugees on U.S. communities. Accordingly, common misperceptions can be effectively addressed. Moreover, the important contributions of immigrants and refugees to U.S. society are provided. New American Economy (2019) lists the realities that run contrary to misconceptions and media portrayals, including the high rates of entrepreneurship among refugees and immigrants, contributions as wage earners and taxpayers, the willingness to build lives in the United States, and how refugees and immigrants are revitalizing locations that have experienced population declines.

Alleman and Brophy (2010) reason social studies should retain a position central to the elementary social studies curriculum. They warn against inadequate approaches and ineffective social studies integration. Shear et al. (2018) assert that children benefit from the promotion and support of anti-oppressive education. They maintain social studies for children has been discounted during an age of standardization. More than ever, there is a need for educators and their students to listen to those with differing opinions of their own as they consider the most pressing issues of our times. Shear et al. (2018) recommend collective, intersectional elementary social studies teachers and students empowered to take action both locally and globally.

CONCLUSION

With the outbreak of the COVID-19 virus and its short-term and potential long-term impact on our educational systems, it is more important now than ever to reject continuing attempts to de-emphasize social studies education. Conversely, dynamic social studies and border pedagogy, energize content and promote healthy discourses on the constantly changing issues facing educators, students, and their families. In essence, the pandemic era is a time of uncertainty for humanity, but border pedagogy provides a pragmatic hope within our predicament. Thus, educators should be afforded opportunities for reflection on our current goals and mission in elementary schools. Border pedagogy also allows for a reimagining of current notions on standardized education, and a reconsideration of the devaluing of social studies content. Border pedagogy provides spaces for the discussion of controversial, current issues such as immigration, refugees, and worker permits. As educators, we need to guide our students in the development of essential questions and a contemplation of how to develop possible resolutions for problems in our society. Students must be provided with the opportunities to confront these issues themselves as part of their journey toward becoming enlightened contributors whose voices can, ultimately, be heard. This study reveals how border pedagogy in elementary school classrooms can promote broader, more in-depth teaching and learning of social studies concepts. As such, border pedagogy bestows upon students opportunities for making local and global connections.

Chapter 11

In Pursuit of Comparative Pedagogies

INTRODUCTION

Recent domestic and international events have reinforced the need for effective transborder dialogue, negotiations, and educational exchanges. By taking these paths possibilities for a pragmatic hope exist. Moreover, these efforts culminate in a critical border praxis (see chapter 7). Comparative perspectives and pedagogical approaches augment informed viewpoints and make possible connections among local, place-based intelligences and more global understandings. According to Mignolo (2012), border thinking is transdisciplinary, transnational, transformational, and "working toward redressing the subalternization of knowledges and the coloniality of power" (p. 338). Alexander (2018b) emphasizes teacher dialogue that encourages, facilitates, questions, and broadens student communications, and recommends the following:

> There should be equal attention to the quality of teacher and pupil talk, and to the agency of others, fellow pupils as well as teachers, in the latter. But unlike several other approaches it eschews the view that there is one right way to maximize the power of classroom talk. (p. 1)

Within educational environs, teachers develop and promote a broad repertoire of pedagogical skills and strategies that ultimately expand and refine the repertoires and capacities of their students. Alexander (2018a) provides a framework for dialogic teaching that is broken down into the following repertoires: interactive modes within classrooms, everyday types of classroom discourses, ways of promoting classroom learning, various forms of motivational language, questioning strategies, and extension activities. Alexander (2018b) also explicates seven justifications for "ethical" education, namely the following broad categories:

1) communicative,
2) social,
3) cultural,
4) political/civic,
5) psychological,
6) neuroscientic, and
7) pedagogical. (p. 4)

Alexander (2018b) posits that within educational settings, "collectivity, reciprocity and supportiveness characterize the classroom culture and pattern of relationships within which dialogue is most likely to prosper, its learning potential has the best chance of being realized, and students will be most at ease in venturing and discussing ideas" (Alexander, 2018b, p. 6).

Bakhtin (1981) describes dialogue as a perpetual, ongoing process that moves the center of discourses from the teacher-centered, or traditional classroom instruction, to student voices and how the teachers respond to those student voices. Discourses, including language, actions, thoughts, histories, and silence are so much a part of daily lives that we fail to be aware of the background and subsequent impact of our dialogue.

According to Mignolo (2012), border thinking should play an important role in our discourses, whether in educational settings or as a part of institutions and policy-making agendas. Accordingly, it works "toward redressing the subalternization of knowledges and the coloniality of power" (Mignolo, 2012, p. 338). In this manner, current norms of scholarship can be reshaped. He argues for the following:

> Remapping new world order implies remapping cultures of scholarship and the scholarly loci of enunciation from where the world has been mapped. The crisis of "area studies" is the crisis of old borders, be they nation borders or civilization borders. It is also the crisis of the distinction between hegemonic (discipline-based knowledges) and subaltern (area-based knowledges), as if discipline-based knowledges are geographically disincorporated. (Mignolo, 2012, p. 310)

According to Mignolo (2012), border thinking develops from a subaltern perspective and is based on local histories interacting with global designs. In this manner, hegemony and the homogeneity of global designs are challenged.

Mignolo (2012) describes "diversality as a universal project, which means that people and communities have the right to be different precisely because we are all equals" (p. 311). Subaltern voices must be heard, heeded, empowered, and recognized as challenges to world educational, economic, and other hegemonic interests.

COMPARATIVE EDUCATION

The promotion of well-informed, inquiring, highly reflective participant roles within this diversality is an objective of comparative education. Comparative education, in its critical form, plays a vital role in promoting diversality. According to Philips and Schweisfurth (2006), two important purposes of comparative inquiry are to (1) learning from the experiences of others and (2) using what is learned to improve conditions (either abroad or at home). Bereday (1964) argues the two most important components of comparative education are understanding others and better understanding ourselves. According to Bereday, the attraction of contemplating and understanding differences is what compels those with an interest in comparative education. Bereday's model characterizes comparative education as the following:

1. it conceptualizes and represents the essential initial attempts in any investigation to identify the research questions and to "neutralize" them from any particular context;
2. it entails the description of educational phenomena in the countries to be investigated with full attention paid to the local context in terms of its historical, geographical, cultural, political, religious, linguistic features;
3. it involves an attempt to isolate differences through direct comparison of the phenomena observed or the date collected. How different or similar is the data;
4. it comprises explanation through the development of hypotheses;
5. it engages in a reconceptualization and contextualization of the findings; and
6. it consists of application or a generalizability of the findings.

Halls (1990) describes comparative education as an attempt to provide understandings of the characteristics and relationships among institutions. The field of study considers interactions in educational settings and seeks to determine relationships between education and society. Moreover, comparative education sets out to relate educational change to education philosophy. Halls believes the determination of truths must be accomplished through analogical processes of analyzing similarities and dissimilarities through investigations of both what is considered "known" versus the unknown.

A key component of comparative education is comparative pedagogy. According to Alexander (2009), pedagogy is an aspect of comparative education which demands extensive knowledge of countries being investigated, including the cultures, systems, and policies of those countries. Alexander (2009) provides defines pedagogy as such:

> (It) is the observable act of teaching together with its attendant discourse of Educational theories, values, evidence and justifications. It is what one needs to know, and the skills one needs to command, in order to make and justify the many different kinds of decisions of which teaching is constituted. (p. 9)

Comparative pedagogy, as noted by Alexander (2009), "identifies, explores, and explains similarities and differences in pedagogy, as concept, discourse and practice, across designated units of comparison such as nation states" (p. 4). Comparative pedagogy discovers and explicates both the universals and the culturally and geographically particulars. In this manner, pedagogic theory and pedagogic practice, in turn, are informed and extended.

Alexander (2009) offers three conditions for a comparative pedagogy. First, it should incorporate a defensible rationale and methodology for comparing across sites, cultures, nations and/or regions. Second, it should combine procedures for studying teaching empirically with ways of accessing the values, ideas, and debates which inform, shape, and explain it. Third, because these values, ideas and debates are part of a wider educational discourse and—typically—are located in the context of public national education systems as well as schools and classrooms, a comparative pedagogy should access these different levels, contexts and constituencies and examine how they relate to each other and inform the discourse of pedagogy and the act of teaching (p. 4).

Pedagogy is shaped by national culture and history, and by the migration of ideas and practices across national borders, as well as by more immediate practical exigencies and constraints such as policy and resources.

Alexander (2009) investigated teachers in five nations and subsequently articulated, enacted, or questioned three versions of human relations that were referred to as *individualism, community,* and *collectivism.* Each version is described as follows:

1. *Individualism* puts self above others and personal rights before collective responsibilities.
    It emphasizes unconstrained freedom of action and thought.
2. *Community* centers on human interdependence, caring for others, sharing and collaborating.
3. *Collectivism* also emphasizes human interdependence, but only in so far as it serves the larger needs of society, or the state (the two are not identical), as a whole (Alexander, 2009, p. 12).

Therefore, the ultimate goals of comparative education include reflecting upon, reexamining, and contextualizing pedagogy, human relations, and educational environments. Alexander (2009) maintains, "A properly-conceived comparative pedagogy can both enhance our understanding of the interplay of education and culture and help us to improve the quality of educational provision" (p. 14).

Tatto (2011) argues for comparative research that is collaborative, reflective, rigorous, capacity building, and policy oriented. Accordingly, comparative research needs to allow for organic learning and produce usable knowledge for policy making and subsequent implementation. A comparative-collaborative-reflective approach to policy-oriented inquiry is necessary for the creation spaces for the joint construction and contextualization of policy-usable knowledge. Agency must be promoted and local considerations must be valued. Tatto (2011) puts forth that "comparative research is uniquely positioned to create spaces for the collaborative construction and collaborative contextualization of reflective, policy-usable knowledge" (p. 511). Policy makers and educators too often look outside their locales without considering how to adapt and reimagine how to effectively resolve complex, unique, and local educational problems.

Researchers in comparative education must take on the responsibilities for illuminating and contemplating possible solutions for multifaceted issues. It is often the cultural, contextual, structural, and functional aspects of education systems that are so dissimilar as to provide motivations for comparison, and it is the evident contrasts that frame rationale and research questions to better analyses of differences in rituals, cultural norms, and educational expectations. Phillips and Schweisfurth (2006) observe, "Once criteria have been established for the task of comparison. and data have been compared and contrasted, attempts to postulate explanations for differences or similarities can begin" (p. 99).

The following description of comparative education is provided by Phillips and Schweisworth (2006):

Comparative education is a very broad area within the huge range of topics and research approaches subsumed under "educational studies." There can be no single approach to comparison that will be agreed upon or that will be appropriate even to the majority of circumstances. But, at the very least there should be attempts to produce a systematic framework for analysis which uses techniques of what Bereday (1964) called juxtaposition of data for comparison and which includes a full consideration of context in any attempts to reach conclusions or to generalize from the findings. (p. 101)

Comparative and international education forms a symbiotic relationship. Philips and Schweisfurth (2006) note "comparative education without the 'international' qualifier might be comparing anything: two learners in one classroom; three textbooks in one subject. International education without comparison denies its intellectual foundations" (p. 152).

Comparative education should take on the role of keeping politicians, administrators, and media commentators in check. These are individuals who, in certain cases, put forth their positions in public spheres and make important decisions on subjects with little empirical evidence and data. Thus, it is incumbent on scholars engaged in transnational and comparative education to counter those claims. Comparative education can and should have a moral purpose as well as an academic or practical one. Philips and Schweisfurth (2006) maintain, "The study of education without a comparative dimension is the poorer for it; thinking and engaging internationally is a prerequisite for all serious scholarship and research. Combining both is the task of everyone involved in a field which becoming increasingly important to sustain and develop in our globalized world" (p. 157).

An important part of comparative educational research is the analysis of discourses embedded within various contexts. Discourses include language, actions, thoughts, histories, and silence. Discourses inform on why we think certain ways. Discourse analysis educates us on how we evaluate and value others and their ideas. Discourses are so deeply rooted in our everyday lives that we fail to recognize the power and shaping of most of them. Critical discourse analysis, in turn, brings to light issues of power, manipulation, exploitation, and structural inequities in education, media, and politics. This approach follows on Freire (1995) recommendations for deciphering both local and global surroundings, to "to perceive social, political, and economic contradictions, and to take action against the oppressive elements of reality" (p. 17). In this manner, educators become cultural workers.

Border pedagogy and comparative education intersect when comparative educational research methodologies and critical discourse analysis are employed within transborder and transnational contexts. The border metaphor invites us to identify and map the multidimensional boundaries that simultaneously enable and constrain students' learning. Moreover, concepts of borderlands promote awareness of the uncertainties and intricacies of these ever-changing environs. Critical postmodern perspectives inform us that knowledge is continually being formed and reformed in response to evolving situations. Critical postmodernism points to the interconnections of identity, thought, and culture in learning. In this manner, new ideas promote creative change and possibilities, essential for participation in a democratic society. A border pedagogy allows for the recognition of opportunities for confronting and resolving inequities of power and authority. Border theory informs us of how institutions contribute to a reproduction of knowledge and challenges these assumptions. Paasi (2011) describes border theory as any valid contextual theorization of boundaries should combine at least such processes, practices and discourses such as the production and reproduction—or institutionalization—of territoriality/territory, state power, human agency and human experience. These practices are normally institutionalized, involve both formal and informal institutions, and may be deeply symbolized. (p. 31)

Paasi (2011) describes practices incorporating border theory as "rarely only local, but may have their origin and constitutive power at a distance, on various *scales* (which are not fixed), from local to global" (p. 31). Hence, it is crucial that comparative research builds upon knowledge and understandings of local contexts and draws comparisons of those conditions to larger regional, national, and transnational contexts.

COMPARATIVE EDUCATION IN SELECTED U.S. CONTEXTS

Acknowledgment of local, state, and national contexts for comparisons are requisite for better understandings of practices within one's own perspectives and understandings of views held outside of those bordered surroundings. Lindaman and Ward (2004) assert that within the past two to three decades the following has occurred within the contexts of the U.S. educational system:

> Textbook publishers in the US have become averse to bold historical narratives for fear of being labeled as too liberal, too conservative, too patriotic, or too sexist and rendering themselves unattractive to buyers on the textbook market. To meet the market's demands, textbook publishers are eliminating perspective, interpretation, historiography, bias, debate, and controversy. By reducing history to a series of inoffensive facts and figures, no matter how attractively packaged, publishers are effectively judging students incapable of discussing and debating important topics and issues. (p. xx)

As the United States developed within a global context for most of its history, as opposed to within isolationist milieus, other nations must be considered for their economic, societal, cultural, and historical connections with the United States. In most cases, global connections are only addressed within the context of the impact of the U.S. foreign policy or from the viewpoint of U.S. interests.

Comparative history is relatively new in the United States (Lindaman & Ward, 2004) and, increasingly relevant to recent educational, economic, political, and historical developments. Lindaman and Ward (2004) argue that despite the fact we have the technological access to learn about other cultures and societies, U.S. educational systems fall short in providing understandings of the rest of the world. Another oversight and limitation within the U.S. curriculum is teaching and learning how other countries' educational systems view the United States and its policies.

U.S. and Mexico Border Contexts

To use the U.S. and Mexico border as a case in point, Cervantes-Soon (2012) and Valenzuela (1999) point out that Latinx students in the United States, as well as other students of color and low socioeconomic background, often face deficit views (Valencia, 2010) and have been denied opportunities to engage in their own histories and educational development. According to Cervantes-Soon (2012), Latinx students "have and continue to experience political violence and marginalization in schools and in society in general due to racism, classism, patriarchy, and linguistic discrimination among many other things" (p. 387). All too often the students' potential contributions are discounted, devalued, and ignored. Within their funds of knowledge are intelligences developed and honed due to their experiences as border-crossers, which provides them with unique abilities to traverse, persist, and overcome daily challenges within their multilingual, diverse cultural, and multiple-identity environs (Cervantes-Soon, 2012; González et al., 2005).

Cervantes-Soon (2012) recommends the implementation of *testimonios* as a pedagogical practice to facilitate and document students' and teachers' lived experiences, narratives, and knowledge. In this manner, there is pragmatic hope for creating and providing empowering learning for Latinx and other students of color. *Testimonios* enable students to create and produce both organically and situated in the contexts of students' daily realities. According to Cervantes-Soon (2012),

> The methodological concerns of *testimonio* are often around giving voice to silences, representing the other, reclaiming authority to narrate, and disentangling questions surrounding legitimate truth. Most of the methodological and epistemological discussions regarding *testimonios* focus on an approach in which an interlocutor, who is an outside activist and/or ally, records, transcribes, edits, and prepares a manuscript for publication. Within this approach, a *testimonialista* works closely with the recorder/researcher/journalist to bring attention to her community's experiences. When translating, for example, terms of endearment, underlying meaning can get lost in translation. One must be cautious to translate conceptually rather than literally because in translating particular terms, nuances get lost, and we run the risk of reproducing language marginalization. Translating *testimonios* from Spanish into English includes translating culturally-specific knowledge that can shift meaning and

reproduce negative connotations associated with gendered or racialized terms of endearment. (p. 387)

Historical Contexts of U.S./Mexico Relations

To better comprehend the disparate perspectives of the U.S./Mexico shared histories and current issues between the two political, economic, and cultural entities it betters one's overall comprehension of the two countries intertwined histories and involvements. Lindaman and Ward (2004) point out the following:

> Through a combination of political diplomacy and military might, the US was able to expand its own borders at the expense of its Mexican neighbor during the 19th century. US textbooks speak of the "annexation" of Texas, but Mexican texts view the loss of territory as a chapter in the history of American imperialism. (p. 72)

The Treaty of Guadalupe Hidalgo put an end to the war between the United States and Mexico. The accord was signed February 2, 1848. The treaty granted occupation rights to the United States in the territories of Texas, New Mexico, Upper California, and the northern part of Tamaulipas, Coahuila, and Sonora. The northern frontier of Mexico would be the Rio Bravo. Moreover, the U.S. government agreed to pay the claims of its citizens against the Mexican government. It would not demand any compensation for the expenses of war. It would pay 15 million pesos for the territories obtained and would prevent incursions from barbaric Indians. Mexico remained plunged in a crises that unleashed new internal conflicts. The country lost an area of 2.4 million km., more than half its territory, in signing the Treaty of Guadalupe Hidalgo. Moreover, the demands of the United States did not end. In December 1853, they demanded the cession of the Baja California territory, at the northern border of the country, and the Tehuantepec Pass, but the Mexican representatives rebuffed such aspirations. However, Santa Anna sold the territory of La Mesilla (109,574 km.) for 10 million pesos, of which the U.S. Congress only agreed to pay 7 million (p. 77).

More recently, free trade agreements were supposed to bring promised economic growth to Mexico, but after 1994 Mexico suffered new economic crises, including harsh devaluation of the Mexican peso.

U.S./Canada Contexts

U.S. textbooks often see the War of 1812 as a minor war, and U.S. textbooks blame Great Britain for the cause of the war. Lindaman and Ward (2004) argue the broader European context out of which the War of 1812 began rarely receives a footnote in U.S. history. Accordingly, Napoleon was dominating Europe at the time. French armies controlled much of the European continent, yet Napoleon was locked in a battle on land and sea with England, France's traditional enemy.

Canadian textbooks attach "special significance to the War of 1812," a war in which Canada was invaded by the United States (Lindaman & Ward, 2004). The outcome of the War of 1812 had a strong impact on Canada, particularly. A struggle between British and American allegiance was resolved as the British retained their influence on Upper Canada, and U.S. political influence declined. According to Lindaman and Ward (2004),

> Hostilities ended in 1814, and the results of the peace negotiations were summarized by the Treaty of Ghent. A major portion of the boundary between the US and British territory was clarified. Because of the war, large scale American immigration into the colony came to an end. After 1815 Americans could not get land grants, and new rulings made it difficult for them to obtain titles of property. (Lindaman & Ward, 2004, p. 54)

Another outcome of the War of 1812 was the growth of Canadian nationalism. The war gave Upper Canada a history, and anti-U.S. sentiments became an important ingredient. Loyalists who remained faithful to the British government witnessed the burning and looting of their possessions and were driven into exile by those who supported the American Revolution. For those who fought for Upper Canada they were proud of their successful defense of their homeland from U.S. attacks and attempted takeovers.

Moreover, throughout Canada's history anti-American sentiment has been revived by changes in the American economic policy that send major shock waves through the Canadian economy. Accordingly, in 1969 former prime minister Pierre Trudeau described Canada's uncomfortable dependence on the U.S. economy, "Living next to you is in some ways like sleeping with an elephant. No matter how friendly and even-tempered is the beast, if I can call it that, one is affected by every twitch and grunt" (Lindaman & Ward, 2004, p. 55). Trudeau's pronouncement became famous and accurately reflected and predicted the positions of Canadians on numerous occasions after his comments were uttered.

Immigrant Education in Australian Contexts

Border crossings as a metaphor has also been applied in non-U.S. research settings. For example, Amigó (2017) examines the shortcomings of multicultural education, especially as it applies to indigenous, immigrants, and minority groups in Australia. Although multicultural approaches purport to promote diversity within educational settings, critics note that discussions of class, institutionalized racism, and capitalism are lacking (Banks, 2009). Amigó (2017) also notes that current approaches "overlooks immigrant families' own projects in relation to the education of their children, and in particular, how diasporic public spheres affect parental aspirations in relation to educational processes" (p. 149). All too often, in an Australian context the primary effects of schooling on immigrant, indigenous, and minority group students are socialization and acculturation.

Liddicoat (2009) describes how the policy focus in 1970s Australia centered on tolerance and acceptance of *others*, while in the 1980s educational policies concentrated more on the importance of diversity as advantageous for Australia's increasingly international economy. The focus on multicultural education with a globalized economy deepened in the 1990s, but there was a shift toward more assimilationist ideologies in the 2000s. Accordingly, Liddicoat (2009) and Hage (1998) maintain Australia's prevailing concerns have been for maintaining the dominant, mainstream culture as at the heart of Australia's linguistic and cultural identities, although multiculturalism was still being touted as part of the national economic agenda. To the contrary, Isik-Ercan (2014) puts forth immigrant parents and children retain their identities to jointly shape hybrid spaces and third spaces (Bhabha, 2004). This corresponds with border-crossers of the U.S. and Mexico border establishing agency and hybrid identities, or nepantla (Anzaldua, 2002). The need to create third spaces in Australia run parallel with what Anzaldua (1987) describes as the generating of bridges to crossing liminal spaces that connect worlds. Maffie (2007) states that nepantla is rooted in a belief system that border crossings take place within "a dynamic zone of mutual transaction, confluence, unstable and diffuse identity, and transformation" (p. 16).

In an Australian context, Amigó (2017) recommends a greater awareness that schools of the "complex and critical processes that immigrant families go through, including the development of hybrid identities and immigrant parents' drive to maintain their heritage" (p. 159). Educational curriculum and policies should address diversity in ways more engaged and inclusive to improve the education of immigrants, indigenous children, and minority groups within Australia. There is a need for the educational system to better prepare students with understandings of interconnected and highly mobile populations, along with the issues and problems facing those who are not part of the dominant society. Multilingualism and cross-cultural communication should be highly valued. In this manner, Australian educational systems must embrace opportunities to promote social change (Amigó, 2017).

As noted in the comparative contexts of the United States, Mexico, Canada, and Australia cross border dialogue and transnational pedagogical approaches provide enriched and engaging understandings of historical, political, economic, social, and cultural differences within and across spaces. Rather than discourage broadened perspectives of shared situations and contexts, we should inspire and empower learning that was previously overlooked and discounted.

Chapter 12

Emergent Third Spaces

INTRODUCTION

In an era of autocratic leadership and governments, a legitimate concern of educators, cultural workers, and policy makers is how to surmount seemingly incessant contentious unilateral decisions, policy changes, cacophony, intentional distractions, and disregarded dissonance. On the other hand, conflict resolution remains a key component of pragmatic hope and transborder dialogue. Dialogic processes have been dismissed, and proponents of democracy are left reeling and contemplating the rise of such populist and nationalist movements within their own borders. Recent history has given the rise of more ego-driven and authoritarian-style world leaders in Saudi Arabia, North Korea, the Philippines, Turkey, Russia, Brazil, Iran, China, the United States, and the United Kingdom, among others. These developments stand in direct contrast to the notion of strong governance epitomized by leading through example for the common good. Leaders, themselves, have abandoned notions of modeling behaviors for their constituents. Democracy, especially, for underrepresented and minority groups within authoritarian countries, loses any sort of consideration and significant segments of the overall population feel disillusioned and powerless in their abilities to affect change. Puigvert notes how anti-democratic movements block meaningful change and are, consequently, problematic. According to Puigvert (2012, p. 93),

> Dismissing the role of dialogue in the analysis of societies and the possibility to transform them, means undertaking partial and biased analyses—it means dismissing the capacity of citizens to reflect on society, analyze it, decide on it, and transform it. It also entails resignation to the power structures that will persist if the role of dialogue is not recognized and emphasized. Intellectuals

can no more claim themselves as making deep analysis of social processes while denying this evidence. (p. 93)

On the contrary, effective dialogue should play a more central role educational, economic, and governmental institutions. Puigvert (2012) recommends strengthening the role of dialogue in the academic context by incorporating it into the research process. Furthermore, there is a need for studies that identify and analyze the barriers obstructing broader implementation of dialogue in overall society, as well as how to challenge and overcome those impediments.

Social actors through participatory and deliberative processes develop a sense of empowerment and agency. The incorporation of dialogue in the public and private spheres has promoted conscious efforts to transform violence and aggression into dialogue and consensus. For example, dialogic relations are constructed through social consensus and have been found to address gender violence (Puigvert, 2012). The roles of academic and social theory in dialogic processes are to inform social action and collaborate with social actors.

As a case in point, Leon-Guerrero et al. (2019) reported on an organization entitled Since 1997 Community Dialogue (CD) that has facilitated interactions crossing social borders in Northern Ireland since 1997. A core dialogue facilitator community exists in Northern Ireland with CD as one organization within that community. The dialogue facilitator community has a shared understanding of dialogue and the significance of empathetic understanding within it. CD in an organization that has adopted an approach to dialogue forged from its inception, and on processes involving facilitators as valuable resources "in a post-violent-conflict society" (Leon-Guerrero et al., 2019, p. 9). Facilitators were asked to reflect on their work and, accordingly, offered a self-appraisal of dialogue's capacity to make a positive difference in the lives of the CD participants from various religious and socioeconomic backgrounds. The facilitators of CD reported the effects of dialogue "can be visible and invisible, immediate and longer-term, and can lead to something new as the result of the process generating human connections where they had not existed before" (Leon-Guerrero et al., 2019, p. 8).

Leon-Guerrero et al. (2019) found that policy makers often overlook dialogue as a strategy for creating a healthy society at least in part because, by definition, it employs smaller-scale, face-to-face community, and peace building. Several facilitators made the point that substantive, long-term consequences cannot be measured adequately by collecting short-term data, which are called outcomes or results by funders and usually are determined by counting the number of participants, among other deliverables. It is the interviewees' contention as well as ours that assessing the more substantial impact of dialogue requires innovative evaluative studies that would need to include dialogue participants and longitudinal data. Additionally, CD facilitators spoke of the urgent need for follow-up activities to dialogue, with one facilitator offering, "We are good at opening the boxes, but we don't do anything with them." Facilitators recommended offering participants in CD dialogue further support and assistance in fostering and sustaining the interpersonal connections developed during the dialogue sessions. Moreover, facilitators noted that funding was needed for the design and maintenance of local projects designed to reduce conflict and violence and promote human thriving in their communities. To the contrary, facilitators reported diminishing resources are being committed to sustaining dialogue and CD organizational efforts. Despite evidence of successes for CD, both short term and longer term, future financial support was still in question, a situation facilitators found discouraging. They expressed concerns for a return to "the deeply destructive and ingrained cultural practice of silencing" and a perpetuation of existing problematic and "polarizing stereotypes and social stagnation" (Leon-Guerrero et al., 2019, p. 10).

Leon-Guerrero et al. (2019) note that processes of dialogue reveal perspectives on long-standing and deeply divisive issues, fears, and concerns often intentionally sidestepped in the regular course of human interaction. Their recommendations were for continuing the work of dialogue in Northern Ireland. Furthermore, the findings of their investigations advocate that public policy recognized and reinforce the value of the dialogue network in Northern Ireland. In this manner, the extent and impact of its work should receive more national and transnational attention. Accordingly, the wisdom, knowledge, and skill of the CD community of practitioners needs to be passed on systematically to a next generation of facilitators, as thirteen of the nineteen facilitators in this study were over fifty years of age (Leon-Guerrero et al., 2019).

On the larger world stage, our past and existing structures for dialogic processes should be continually examined and reevaluated. Within these contexts, purportedly democratic nations participate, preside over, intercede, and make decisions on transnational dialogue. Daase (2006) puts forth countries that consider themselves democracies, including the United States and the United Kingdom, hold institutionalized dispositions that, at times, prevent them from mediating in conflict. Thus, "they dampen conflicts between democracies by instilling trust through shared values, but they can provoke conflicts between democracies and non-democracies. Especially if democracy is seen as a universal right that should be spread globally through regime change, democracy can become a cause of war" (Daase, 2006, p. 83). The U.S. and U.K. governments, under the guise of promoting democracy, proved this point when they delegitimized, demonized, and invaded Iraq in

2003. By "doing so, they falsified an old assumption in political science, namely that democracies do not wage preventive wars" under false pretenses (Daase, 2006, p. 83).

Ultimately, human rights education (HRE) must be a priority of educational, policy-making, and political dialogue. Tibbitts and Katz (2018) note that although more than eighty-three countries worldwide have adopted HRE in some form, there are questions of whether HRE messages and approaches are "becoming diluted, or even coopted, by state interests" (p. 33). Moreover, there are concerns of superficial commitments and the undermining of the emancipatory nature of HRE. Questions of how human rights projects, conceived in Western culture and hegemonic in its approach with universal values and norms, can be compatible with local cultures and sufficiently concerned with the everyday lives of individuals and communities in non-Western cultures. Tibbetts and Katz (2018) maintain,

> A strong critique of a traditional transmission approach to HRE is that it does not allow learners to consider these concerns, thereby contributing to a non-reflective socialization process. At best, such an HRE approach fails to fully foster the critical capacities of learners; at worst, this form of HRE promotes a hegemonic, Western-centered values system. These concerns are also amplified in environments with a political sensitivity to the term "human rights," for reasons related to local political dynamics. (p. 33)

HRE theorists have embraced critical pedagogy, including the teachings of Freire (2005), as foundational to HRE. Accordingly, the social and cultural environments of learners must considered and, at the same time, the human rights framework must be continually reevaluated. In this manner, learners are allowed and encouraged to consider hegemonic influences so that they become empowered to promote and protect human dignity. In this manner, best approaches to HRE can be discussed, and ultimately determined. Thus, "rather than simply applying a universal set of abstract principles, adherents actively interpret, shape, and transform rights. In every learning context, HRE pedagogy needs to embody listening and dialogue" (Tibbetts & Katz, p. 33).

As it stands, gulfs exist among the viewpoints held by proponents of HRE pedagogy and official state positions. Conflict exists between the "emancipatory roots of HRE and the lived educational policies and practices of states and schools" (p. 34). All too often institutionalized policies, including those that determine curricula, teacher preparation, and educational resources stand in the way of human rights learning in classrooms.

The time is long overdue for a cross-border praxis that involves the incorporation of heteroglossia, meliorism, nepantla, dialogic feminism, critical cosmopolitanism, and pragmatic hope as part of a critical border praxis, as discussed in previous chapters. Central to this praxis are border crossings and, ultimately, conceptualizations, development, and implementations of newly emergent third spaces. Bhabha (2004) developed third space theory, an explication of how each person's unique being is formed through hybridity. Hybridity involves the contextualized intersections of culture found in one's identity. Hybridity demonstrates how cultures come to be represented by processes of iteration and translation through which identities attempt to be defined by those around us. This contrasts with any thoughts of the purity of cultures which can become political arguments for the hierarchy and the ascendancy of particular cultures (Bhabha, 2004). Bhabha includes interpretations of hybridity as a part of postcolonial discourses. Accordingly, hybridity is a strategic reversal of the processes of domination through disavowal. Hybridity counters assumptions of colonial identity rendered by those in power and through discrimination. Hence, understanding concepts of hybridity is important for challenging continuing demands of colonial power, while re-identifying those who have been colonized and discriminated against by reversing the focus of the discriminated back upon the colonizer (Bhabha, 2004). In U.S. contexts, the Black Lives Movement seeks to precipitate social and create hybrid, third spaces where none had previously existed.

As dialogue is essential to the promotion, development, facilitation, and praxis of third spaces, it is beneficial that we consider how dialogue is deemed "effective." Dialogue processes are never simple nor straightforward, as indeed facilitators of dialogue must make salient and address the intricacies underlying existing conflicts and points of contention. Leon-Guerrero et al. (2019) clarify some of the characteristics of effective dialogic processes based on how dialogue facilitators reported on their experiences and knowledge construction with the CD Organization in Northern Ireland, a part of the UK beset with religious and socioeconomic strife as well disputes as the result of its partition from the Republic of Ireland, its neighbor to the south. Facilitators of CD in Northern Ireland emphasized the following characteristics as essential dialogue practices (Leon-Guerrero et al., 2019):

- Active, deep, respectful listening;
- dialogue with flexible agendas, participant-led with tact and sensitivity to the potentially polemical topics;
- promotion of a safe space where dialogue participants are empowered to speak freely and openly while engaging with each other, including a conscientious arrangement of the physical environment and organizational socialization;
- expectations for strong facilitator preparation prior to dialogue sessions, opportunities for consultation among facilitators during ongoing sessions,

and for dialogue participants to be informed of expectations upfront and beforehand;
- incorporating humor as an integral part of building group awareness, dynamics, and trust; and
- establishing consensus after receiving participant input on ground rules for dialogue sessions, which requires facilitators to encourage responsibility, openness, respectful interaction, and confidentiality.

Third space theory emerges from the sociocultural approaches promoted by Vykotsky (1962), which is immersed in the role of culture in the mind, and how the mind develops by incorporating shared artifacts that produce knowledge within a culture over time. Bhabha (2004) applies sociocultural approaches directly to postcolonial spaces where unequal and uneven forces of cultural representation still exist.

Within discourses of dissent, third space can be interpreted as either (1) a space where the oppressed plot their liberation or (2) a space where oppressed and oppressor are able to come together and removes themselves of oppression, even if that space only exists in that particular moment in time (Bhabha, 2004). Bhabha, however, advocates for enduring change in the following statement:

> What is crucial to . . . such a vision of the future is the belief that we must not merely change the narratives of our histories, but also transform our sense of what it means to live, to be, in other times and spaces, both human and historical. (2004, p. 367)

Soja (2009), as a postmodern political geographer, applies Bhabha's concepts more directly to the social sciences, and refers to those interpretations as "third space." Soja's work was influenced by the work of French urban sociologist Lefebvre, author of *The Production of Space* (1974). Soja is noted for his contributions to spatial theory and the field of cultural geography as he updated Lefebvre's concept of the spatial triad with his own concept of spatial trialectics which includes third space, or spaces that can be real or imagined.

Soja (2009) does not conceptualize third space as an alternative concept to existing approaches. Rather, third space is described as follows:

> It is an invitation to enter a space of extraordinary openness, a place of critical exchange where the geographical imagination can be expanded to encompass a multiplicity of perspectives that have heretofore been considered by the epistemological referees to be incompatible, uncombinable . . . . Third space is rooted in just such a recombinational and radically open perspective. (Soja, 2009, p. 50)

Soja credits Lefebvre (1974) for first using the term "thirdspace." Lefebvre also theorized difference and otherness in explicitly spatial terms and critiqued representations of power and the power of representations. According to Soja (2009), Lefebvre contended that difference be contextualized in social and political practices. Lefebvre argued for a need to struggle for "the right to be different against the increasing forces of homogenization, fragmentation, and hierarchically organized power that defined the specific geography of capitalism" (Soja, 2009, p. 50). Soja also credits Lefebvre (1974) for developing a dialectics of inequalities and differentiation and subsequently creating a space of "collective resistance, a third space of political choice that is also a meeting place for all peripherized or marginalized subjects wherever they may be located" (Soja, 2009, p. 50). Accordingly, it is a political space where new and different forms of citizenship can be defined and realized. Soja also credits Lefebvre for critiques of dualisms in geography that juxtapose first space and second space. Consequently, discourses in geography have failed to "respond adequately to the new developments" (Soja, 2009, p. 50). Thus, there is a pressing need for third spaces. According to Soja,

> Such thirding is designed not just to critique First space and Second space modes of thought but also to reinvigorate their approaches to spatial knowledge with new possibilities heretofore unthought of inside the traditional spatial disciplines. (2009, p. 56)

Third space thinking implies a new view on the world and the production of knowledge. It implies a new spatial awareness which, emerges as a product of a thirding of the spatial imagination, the creation of another mode of thinking about space that draws upon the material and mental spaces of the traditional dualism but extends well beyond them in scope, substance, and meaning.

Soja (2009) describes Bhabha's approach to third space as an example for the understanding of "third space" as a mutual political strategy against all forms of oppression. Bhahbha describes this postcolonial approach as "productive" and differing from "liberal relativist perspectives on cultural diversity and multiculturalism, which form another discursive space" (Soja, 2009, p. 57).

Bhabha (2004) builds upon the postmodern critique of Western modernity to form a case for the postcolonial disruption of that modernity. Schulze-Engler (2009) notes that Bhabha observes the potential for Eurocentricity in the postmodern critique of Western modernity. On the contrary, the postmodern condition should maintain an awareness of the epistemological borders within ethnocentric ideas that have historically limited "other dissonant, even dissident histories and voices—women, the colonized, minority groups, the bearers of policed sexualities" (Schulze-Engler, 2009, p.

129). Hence, Schulze-Engler (2009) maintains "migration, exile and diaspora sets up a peculiar relationship between the postcolonial and the Western nation state" (p. 129).

Schulze-Engler (2009) recommends recognizing the variety of third spaces created in the context of globally interlinked multiple modernities and transnational connections. In this manner, third spaces can arguably contribute towards overcoming a "system that promotes endless rehearsals of Western self-criticism on the one hand and is structurally incapable of perceiving anything but decolonizing narratives in nation states that emerged after decolonization on the other" (p. 139).

Bhabha places third space in the margins and puts forth this social marginality must produce a political strategy to empower and articulate particular goals. Bhabha's conceptualizations are also rooted in the experience of postcoloniality (Soja, 2009). According to this iteration of third space, multiculturalism or diversity of cultures is replaced with cultural hybridity. Soja (2009) notes, "To that end we should remember that it is the 'inter'— the cutting edge of translation and negotiation, the in-between space—that carries the burden of the meaning of culture" (p. 59). Bhabha describes of "going beyond, which means that interventions can modify the existing power relations, if only a Third Space emerges" as the Third Space serves as a "precondition for possible interventions" (Soja, 2009, p. 59). These notions correspond with Soja's recommendations for broadening knowledge, promoting novel critical positions, and developing a new consciousness of space and spatiality.

In border contexts, and certainly not limited to the U.S. and Mexico border, nepantla is a concept that extend ideas of third space. Lizárraga and Gutiérrez (2018) put forth nepantla pedagogies that promote expansive third spaces where students "bring tools, practices, and expertise" from their everyday contexts, including their home and school environments (p. 39). In educational settings, third spaces take the form of well-designed multilingual and multivoiced surroundings as spaces that provide an environment where learners can express themselves and engage more fully. Therefore, nepantla allows for opportunities for reimagining oneself and one's role in society. In this manner, a type of third space emerges in which learners are empowered as agents and contributors to knowledge (Lizárraga & Gutiérrez, 2018).

The creation of efficacious third spaces may, in some cases, require the outside intervention of third parties. Every precaution must be taken to ensure the outside parties have no vested interests in determining how the emergent third space will transpire and materialize. Furthermore, all measures must continue to confirm newly created spaces receive enduring support and feedback. Considerations should be in place for continuing processes of renewal and re-imagination as third spaces are distinguished as non-static in constitution.

Through the aforementioned approaches noted in this chapter we can begin to consider what it looks like to be engaged in border praxis, including the creation and maintenance of third spaces. Problem solving and, ultimately, overcoming obstructions positioned in the path of conflict resolution is an essential part of being involved in dialogue and dialogic processes. Therefore, decision-making processes must attempt to find solutions to essential questions. Those who engage in these processes, yet remain unplacatable and undeterred in their stances, must be informed of consensus decisions. Individuals or entities who continue dissent, despite consensus, must be reassured of future opportunities for dissention, either formal or informal. All of those who are affected by the collective decision-making processes must be reassured of their welcome input and participation in democratic decision making. If necessary, outside sources deemed to be trustworthy and without ulterior motives should be invited and included in processes of formal decision-making processes and diffusing disagreements on the way to creating efficacious third spaces.

It is essential that we conceptualize how this praxis is realized in the context of cross-border educational exchanges, negotiated spatialities, reimagined and re-contextualized platforms for policy makers, and real possibilities for reinvigorated curricula, including teaching and learning. It is through the deconstruction and subsequent, ongoing reconstruction of our professional responsibilities that provide room for informed praxis within these third spaces.

Chapter 13

Conclusion

There Has Never Been a More Crucial Time

RECENT DEVELOPMENTS

In this final chapter of *Promoting Transborder Dialogue During Times of Uncertainty: A Time for Third Spaces,* some key theoretical constructs, as put forth in previous chapters, are part of deliberations. Additionally, chapter 13 considers the implications of recent events for critical praxis and the need for creating third spaces. The necessity of a border praxis that considers meliorism, heteroglossia, nepantla, dialogic feminism, critical cosmopolitanism, and pragmatic hope (as noted in chapters 2–5) persists. The development of third spaces (see chapter 12) is a process that is central to countering courses of action characterized by non-cooperation. Key developments have arisen given the magnitude of recent events in the United States as well as worldwide. This closing chapter will examine some of the impacts of those events and also ask essential questions with regard to how our societies and institutions should process within local, national, and world forums. Moreover, prescient recommendations for current and future struggles in our educational, social, economic, and political spheres will be provided.

In the matter of only a few months inhabitants of the world have experienced seismic alterations to their daily routines, educational systems, and cultural institutions as never experienced in our current lifetimes. Although disease, conflict, and war have brought devastation and hardships to societies previously, this outbreak diverges because the scale, scope, magnitude, and consequences diverge from other misfortunes affecting humanity. At the time of this writing, worldwide approximately 5,000 deaths are being recorded on a daily basis. With the current death totals, it has become impossible to keep up with all of the life stories of the sick, the dead, and families affected by the virus. In parts of the United States and other countries, burial services are hastened with surviving family members not being afforded traditional human interaction and grieving processes. New epicenters of sickness and death are emerging, and talk of a second, even more devastating, COVID-19 viral wave looms on the horizon.

With the aforementioned realities noted, there are other aspects of the pandemic that need consideration. Rapaport (2020, p. 1) puts forth, "Quarantine is a perfect time for reflection." The global pandemic has had profound effects on the educational systems of affected countries nearly worldwide. Face-to-face classes and meetings have been moved to online environs. Decisions have been made to cut budgets in all settings, including schools K-12 and higher education. At a time when transborder dialogue and global interdependence are all the more vital for our co-existence. Rapaport notes,

> There are people who will scapegoat other nations instead of demanding real leadership in their countries. I am concerned that we may hear more and more calls to isolate ourselves, to lock national borders, ignoring the very premise on which this nation was built. I am concerned that, here and there, we see public figures who use the current situation to call for a halt to democratic processes and promote the idea of temporary authoritarian measures; temporary has a tendency to become permanent. (2020, p. 1)

The ongoing COVID-19 pandemic coincides with the proliferation of Black Lives Matter protests around the world. These recent developments reinforce notions of U.S. momentous occurrences precipitating ripple effects, or in some cases, tsunamis in terms of influence worldwide. This situation is reported by some individuals in the European Union as the U.S. relinquishment of its role as a global moral leader (Birnbaum, 2020). Protests have erupted in countries outside the United States such as France, the United Kingdom, Australia, South Africa, and Brazil. War-racked Syria features a mural of George Floyd, the person who died under the knee of a Minneapolis, Minnesota, police office. Indeed, Floyd's death now represents not only the struggles of Black Americans but also the privilege of dominant classes and violence and oppression experienced by subjugated populations worldwide (Birnbaum, 2020).

The Black Lives Matter movement in the United States has forced increasingly diverse societies to reexamine the realities of their colonial legacies and modern-day discrimination. Protesters have connected Floyd's death to police brutality in the United Kingdom, Paris, and Germany. Demonstrations throughout Europe also protest discrimination that denies Black Europeans educational opportunities, housing, and jobs. These European activists contend their governments have failed to effectively recognize the root causes of racism within and across transnational borders. Hence, constituents of European countries with histories of colonization who have denied culpabilities and subsequently promoted race-blind societies now face demands to identify and address racism.

A real-world example of how critical border praxis may come to fruition lies in the U.S. Minneapolis and St. Paul metropolitan area, but not as an idealistic, happily live thereafter scenario. Rather, pragmatic hope for Minneapolis and St. Paul resides in circumstances that require efficacious dialogue, collaboration, problem solving, compromise, conflict resolution, and altruistic leadership.

The mayor of Minneapolis, Jacob Frey, received praise for his swift initial response. The morning after Floyd's death, Frey condemned the officers' actions. Four police officers were fired that day and the following day Frey called for felony charges to file against one of the police officers. The president of the Minneapolis African American Leadership Council, met with Frey and reported, "Mayor Frey was the mayor for all people in this situation" (Berg, 2020). In neighboring St. Paul, the mayor, Melvin Carter, is the city's first Black mayor. Both Frey and Carter campaigned and were elected based on their promises of police reform after both cities have received national attention for fatal police shootings. Both mayors have met both praise and criticism for their varied records of success in implementing police reform.

In Minneapolis, Frey faces an uphill battle in untangling the years of mistrust between the community and police department For further dialogue and support, it has been suggested that Frey engage with Carter, the mayor of Minneapolis' twin city, St. Paul. Carter, whose father is a now-retired police officer and whose mother is a retired educator, has been a proponent of "community-first policing" since being elected mayor of St. Paul, Minnesota (Berg, 2020). Carter offers the following observations with regards to the challenges facing fellow mayor, Frey:

> I think that was an important thing to do and it seems he voices a commitment to fundamentally changing the nature of the Minneapolis Police Department. Clearly there are individuals who feel like that still doesn't go far enough. I think we'll see. I think time will tell. (Berg, 2020)

Prior controversial police shootings influenced Carter's decision to emphasize police reform during his initial St. Paul mayoral election campaign. Philando Castile, a thirty-two-year-old Black man, was shot and killed during a traffic stop by police in a St. Paul suburb the year before Carter was elected in St. Paul. Carter worked with police leadership to completely re-envision and revise the St. Paul Police Department's use-of-force policy (Berg, 2020). As a result, it became an officer's duty to deescalate conflict and intervene in potentially violent situations. Police were trained to respond differently and appropriately in cases of someone who is passively resisting versus situations where an individual is being aggressive and violent toward others. St. Paul also became one of the first agencies in the country to embed social workers alongside police officers to respond to people in crisis (Berg, 2020). Mayor Carter also offers that St. Paul has promoted a model of public safety that goes far beyond policing to be proactive in its approaches to crime prevention.

In 2019, the city passed a community-first public safety proposal that focused on youth jobs and community supports such as ensuring people who return to the community from incarceration can find stable housing. Carter noted the city has been able to accomplish goals without adding a "single police officer" (Berg, 2020). Frey, mayor of Minneapolis, has already indicated that he does not favor "defunding" the police department, but some of the elements of Carter's community-first lens are the same changes advocates are demanding. According to Mayor Carter in St. Paul, "If that's what people are calling for, then it certainly feels like something that we are already doing" (Berg, 2020). Perhaps by paying attention to the St. Paul model, Frey can more readily transitioning from protests to politics in Minneapolis, its sister city. The former mayor of St. Paul from 1990 to 1994, Jim Scheibel, asks,

> How do we make real change? We can march every night, but unless we begin to change the systems, we won't make progress. We really have to dig in and be tenacious about what we want to see happen. And we've got to vote the people out who don't want to listen. (Berg, 2020)

Thus, it is time to develop third spaces where dialogue, especially listening, responding, and taking negotiated actions are possible. Terrill, of the African American Leadership Council, argues that now is the time for real change in Minnesota, in the United States, and worldwide. He states the following:

> If Mr. Floyd's death means anything . . . it shows the rest of the US and the world that Minnesota is not going to have it anymore. Then his death won't be in vain. He would be shocked (if he knew of all the demonstrations taking place). He might have said he'd be OK with it if . . . another Black man or woman doesn't have to suffer the way he did. (Berg, 2020)

The need for international understandings, transborder cooperation, and shared global solutions has never been more pressing. On the contrary, the global pandemic is also an ominous sign of how the lack of emphasis on cross-border dialogue and praxis is detrimental to our societies. There is hope our interconnected societies will learn valuable lessons from the COVID-19 pandemic. Perhaps most important lesson will be the requisite necessity of empowering and transformative education that addresses the needs of a global community (Rapaport, 2020).

According to Tam and El-Azar (2020), the COVID-19 pandemic is reshaping education in the following ways: (1) millions around the globe are educated in new ways; (2) new solutions for education could bring much-needed innovation; but (3) given the digital divide, new education approaches could widen equality gaps. In a matter of weeks, coronavirus (COVID-19) has changed how students, pre-kindergarten through university levels, are educated around the world. By March 13, 2020, the Organization for Economic Co-operation and Development (OECD) estimated that over 421 million children are affected due to school closures announced or implemented in thirty-nine countries. In addition, other countries implemented partial closures. As a result, the situations where millions of students worldwide have continued their school in lockdown and stay-at-home have prompted examples of educational innovation. According to Tam and El-Azar (2020), it has yet to be determined how the long-term effects of COVID-19 will affect education systems, but there are signs suggesting that there will be a lasting impact on the trajectory of innovation and learning in digital environments. However, the real possibilities of permanent budget cuts that affect innovative teaching and learning prevail. There are real possibilities for a widening digital divide, schools finding stop-gap solutions to continue teaching, but the quality of learning is heavily dependent on the level and quality of digital access. With almost 40 percent of the world's population with limited or nonexistent online access, many students, at best, receive lessons and assignments sent via WhatsApp or email. When classes transition online, these children lose out because of the cost of digital devices and data plans. Tam and El-Azar (2020) maintain,

> Unless access costs decrease and quality of access increase in all countries, the gap in education quality, and thus socioeconomic equality will be further exacerbated. The digital divide could become more extreme if educational access is dictated by access to the latest technologies.

As it stands, academic freedom, silenced voices, and funding cutbacks have profoundly impacted educational systems. In the case of the United States, business models for school have replaced child-centered and more humanistic, research-backed approaches to educating our students. Examples of attempts to divert funds for public education to the for-profit education sector proliferate. All too often the families most affected by the reallocation of funding for public, grass roots educational reinvention are intentionally supplied with misinformation and covert processes that cloud the real intentions of those who push for legislated policies that transfer educational funding from populations that stand to benefit the most from additional support for education that is truly in the public interest, as opposed to corporate, opportunist, and narrowly focused special interests. Fischer and Peters (2016) note the following:

> Despite widespread public opposition to the corporate-driven education privatization agenda, at least 172 measures reflecting American Legislative Exchange Council (ALEC) model bills were introduced in 42 states in 2015, according to an analysis by the Center for Media and Democracy, publishers of ALECexposed.org and PRWatch.org.

ALEC was co-founded by conservative activist Paul Weyrich, Henry Hyde—who later became a U.S. congressman, and Lou Barnett—who later became national director of Ronald Reagan's Political Action Committee (Greeley & Fitzgerald, 2011). Weyrich also founded the Heritage Foundation, another conservative think tank. ALEC has been conducting secretive meetings for several years focused on how to profit off and tap into current funding for public education. Koch Industries and the Koch brothers' fortune continue to fund ALEC and their interests are represented in populist-flavored groups entitled the Americans for Prosperity and Freedom Partners. ALEC's Education Task Force is also Koch-funded and works to determine educational policy and legislation. The State Policy Network consists of multiple U.S.-based think tanks and receives its funding from many of the same ALEC represented corporations, foundations, and donor entities (Fischer & Peters, 2016). ALEC's Education Task Force is also funded by the billionaire DeVos family, which included the current U.S. Secretary of Education, Betsy DeVos. ALEC's Education Task Force finances "a privatization operation called American Federation of Children, and by for-profit corporations like K12 Inc., which was founded by junk-bond king Michael Milliken" (Fischer & Peters, 2016). ALEC's Education Task Force has pushed legislation for decades to privatize public schools, weaken teachers' unions, and weaken teacher certification requirements.

ALEC's agenda transforms public education from a public and accountable institution that serves the public into one that serves private, for-profit interests. A common objective of ALEC-sponsored bills is to reinvest taxpayer money from public to private schools through a variety of "voucher" and "tuition tax credit" programs (Fischer & Peters, 2016). ALEC legislation seeks to shift finances and authority from existing educational systems. Fischer and Peters (2016) observe,

The commentary to ALEC's original 1984 voucher bill states that its purpose is "to introduce normal market forces" into education, and to "dismantle the control and power of" teachers' unions by directing money from public institutions to private ones that were less likely to be unionized.

Milton Friedman, economic advisor to President Ronald Reagan, was even more forthcoming in expressing the true intent of ALEC and its agenda during his address to ALEC's 2006 Annual Meeting. He explicitly stated that vouchers are designed to be a step toward "abolishing the public school system" (Fischer & Peters, 2016). Friedman put forth the politically expedient, if covert, way of moving toward an entirely private educational system was through vouchers. ALEC has also been engaged in a relentless attack on teachers, their credentials, and teacher unions. According to Fischer and Peters (2016), ALEC's direct assault on unions has accelerated and continues in the present.

Absenteeism is a recurrent concern in American education, but with the advent of COVID-19 pandemic school buildings are closed and lessons are being conducted remotely. A consequence of these dramatic changes is that more students are missing class by not participating in online educational experiences or not completing assignments (Goldstein et al., 2020). Absence rates are particularly high among low-income students, and some educators report that less than 50 percent of their students are regularly participating in organized instruction. There has been debate on how to address this situation, whether it will lead to additional summer sessions, extended school calendars, or the repetition of coursework once students physically return to classrooms.

Goldstein et al. (2020) report that a subset of students and their parents have completely ceased to communicate with their teachers and schools. Many families have been preoccupied with the broader economic and health effects of the coronavirus outbreak, and there is no longer any sort of involvement or engagement with formal schooling. In this manner, online learning has provided new impediments to learning, particularly with uneven levels of technology and adult supervision. Most notably, there is no precedent in educators' memories for what is happening right now. Schools have weathered disruptive events previously, but earlier adversity consisted of shorter-term uncertainties and affected local areas, as opposed to educational institutions worldwide. At this juncture, educators are uncertain of their responsibilities and risks, as local and state policies are in constant flux. Federal assistance for public education is increasingly limited, as the predominant message conveyed on the national level is to push students back to traditional educational environs, regardless of educators' and family members' concerns for COVID-19 infection.

Educational leaders in various national contexts are engaged in discourses on how to best address current and future obstacles related to the COVID-19 virus. Questions abound on how to ensure the safety and health of students, teachers, staff, administrators, and their families. Dialogue is centered around the various options for maintaining social distancing and sanitization, as well as the promotion of innovative teaching and learning. Preeminent among the concerns is how to successfully reduce the number and interactions of people inside classrooms and buildings at any given time. In essence, the uncertainties are more focused on how to physically distance, rather than social distance, educational communities. There are also major concerns of how to ensure large numbers of students receive all or substantial portions of the current school curriculum that were not successfully completed. Until an efficacious vaccine is available worldwide, extensive testing for COVID-19 cases and follow-up tracing of contacts remain the only options for a continued "flattening the curve," or the caustic optimism associated with spreading out the inevitable vast losses of human life over a period of time. In this manner, the inevitability of infections and deaths remain, but cases are spread out over a longer duration and health care workers are less overwhelmed.

Given the effects of the pandemic and anti-racism movements on educational, economic, and political systems, it is necessary now more than ever for efficacious transnational dialogue and understandings. If anything, the urgency of a border praxis built upon the tenets of meliorism, heteroglossia, nepantla, dialogic feminism, critical cosmopolitanism, and pragmatic hope resonates with increased exigency. Rather than respond to pronouncements of the benefits of unilateralism and isolationist policies, local and global interests must continue to work toward the development of third spaces that advance our current outlooks, reduce our limitations, and inform decision making and policies. Although the most recent push in the United States has been to return to worldviews and protectionist principles that signal a return 1920s U.S. mindsets and realities, including corruption as commonplace, discrimination, xenophobia, widespread racial, and ethnic violence (including a proliferation of lynchings), the burning of places of worship, and "survival-of-the-fittest" attitudes which provided foundations for twentieth-century fascism, both domestically and abroad. Although it is true that history never "truly repeats itself," it should be evident we must consider that times of economic hardship, worldwide cataclysmic challenges, and internal strife resulting from historical injustices and inequities have precluded world wars and conflicts in the past. On the other hand, it is in these very same challenging times that humans have produced significant societal and technological changes. It is during and after these difficult periods that societies have been forced to collectively re-envision and reconsider the possibilities for our institutions.

In terms of meliorism, we must ask ourselves how do we design and facilitate a praxis that improves on coordinated educational and governmental responses to health, safety, security, and social upheavals. Additionally, critical border praxis must include a search for democratic responses to the following questions:

1. What is the role of education in developing understandings of these transnational issues?
2. How can we be proactive so there is a reduction of violence and loss of human lives associated with future pandemics, social unrest, and possible human extinction brought on by climate change?
3. How can our education and preparedness ameliorate conditions associated with pandemics and the unjust conditions in place that demand human rights demonstrations?
4. How can we address systemic prejudice, discrimination, and racism in our educational, economic, political systems?
5. How will current protests and anti-domination protests translate to changes in policy at local, state, national, and transnational levels of government?
6. What is the role of education in developing understandings of these transnational issues?

Therefore, critical border praxis must engage us with essential questions that consider the possibilities for local, national, transnational, global meliorism, and social transformation.

Heteroglossia is crucial for true local, national, and transnational understandings of the concerns of fellow individuals. Efficacious cross-border praxis and communications involve active listening, contemplation, and subsequent responses to the utterances, verbal and non-verbal, of participants in human discourses. Dialectical approaches must engage us in how to put in place effective measures to address the COVID-19 pandemic and future health emergencies, the roots of racism and systemic violence toward Black Americans and non-dominant groups in U.S. society, as well as other pressing issues such as climate change and the real consequences of global warming.

Nepantla serves as a third space for those who have survived colonization and who navigate within a belief system within a borderland, which serves as a dynamic zone of mutual transaction, confluence, hybridity, and transformation. Perspectives of the world are the products of disorder, processes of becoming, and human transitions. As struggle and persistence are a part of daily lives, survivors of nepantla offer knowledge of how to endure periods of uncertainty, whether that time frame is characterized by a deadly pandemic; systemic violence, discrimination, and racism; or environmental destruction caused by human activities.

Dialogic feminism addresses the violence associated with patriarchy a provides us with opportunities for dialogue that demands effectual listening and heeding of all input, concerns, and voices. In this manner, shared social contexts can be re-defined and patriarchy across cultures can be confronted. Dialogic feminism plays an essential role in the development of pragmatic hope for inclusive societies.

Critical cosmopolitanism contrasts with traditional cosmopolitanism in that it engages us with bottoms up, as opposed to top-down, worldviews of educational, social, economic, and political systems. Critical cosmopolitanism counters norms and morality associated with traditional cosmopolitanism and challenges notions of universalism. It focuses on grassroots processes of internal developmental processes rather than hold globalization as most important. Thus, critical cosmopolitanism is post-universalistic and considers the processes through which societies undergo transformation.

Pragmatic hope, as opposed to optimism, considers realistic approaches for the fulfillment of possibilities, meliorism, and social progress. It overrides the smugness of sanguine trust. Pragmatic hope, moreover, involves processes of continual struggle for the realization of ambitions. Accordingly, these hopeful processes require participation and agency as a part of democratic processes. This hope serves as an outgrowth of informed, educated, and reasoned action that seeks to affect societal change.

The rapid spread of COVID-19 has demonstrated the importance of building resilience to face various threats, from pandemic disease to extremist violence to climate insecurity, and even, yes, rapid technological change. The pandemic is also an opportunity to remind ourselves of the skills students need in this unpredictable world such as informed decision making, creative problem solving, and perhaps above all, adaptability. To ensure those skills remain a priority for all students, resilience must be built into our educational systems as well.

We are living in a time when meaningful dialogue and action must readdress, reeducate, reanalyze, reevaluate, relearn, redefine, reimagine, reconceptualize, re-visualize, recommit, repurpose, recreate through critical border praxis. To accomplish these ends there must be a recognition of the gulfs that exist among transnational communications and transborder understandings. In this manner, processes of reconciliation may begin to transpire or continue within our divergent educational, economic, social, and political systems. Major questions remain with regard to the following transnational issues, for example:

At this juncture major questions remain as to how we as part of the "new normal" answer the transnational issues, such as the following (among other concerns as well):

(1) How do we as societies define and address terrorism worldwide, and especially its root causes?
(2) How do we, as different cultures, underscore the multidirectional needs for religious tolerance worldwide?
(3) How can the increasingly essential need for media literacy be taught and realized in an age of strategically manufactured disinformation and outright lies?
(4) How do we continually investigate and provide reparations for the consequences of cultural imperialism and post-colonial policies while simultaneously reducing conduits of corruption and further oppression?

We must address these questions if we are to uncover the root causes of contention and conflict. Moreover, the current time is well-suited for reconsidering the new realm of possibilities for post-pandemic societies. Critical border praxis provides pragmatic hope and opportunities for requisite plans of action during an era of COVID-19 pandemic, Black Lives Matter movements for systemic change, and worldwide confrontation of colonial past leaders and their responsibilities for widespread violence and deaths. It is a time for challenging structural racism associated with the COVID-19 pandemic as opposed to racist notions of why some people are more adversely affected than others. The lack of availability of personal protective equipment, national policy upholding science-based recommendations, and early testing for all Americans are all issues that should not be overlooked along with other pandemic and post-pandemic concerns.

It is time for governments, societies, economic interests, and educational systems to work within the proper balance of collectivism and individualism, without juxtaposing one against the other. Teachers and their students need to be educated so they understand that no society or person can proceed unilaterally or based on their sole interests.

In this manner, dialogic processes and border praxis must lead us down the path of realizing possibilities for meliorism. With this initial realization, there is a promise for reimagining our power relationships and institutions, including educational environments. Critical border praxis is a process that asks us to reconceptualize after we reimagine. Reinvigoration should follow our re-conceptualizations. After reconceptualizing, we must continue our efforts to reinvent our local, state, national, transnational, and world communities. Reinvention must be a part of ongoing reconstruction of structural inequities and injustices. Thus, critical border praxis promotes reactivation, and when we reactive ourselves we also repurpose our lives.

We must contemplate and engage in dialogue and dialectical processes that reexamine our own vulnerabilities yet remain steadfast against an acquiescence and resignation to the notion of the powerful world magnates and corporations rendering the rest of us powerless. If we proceed as educated, informed, and empowered citizenry we can counter fears of losing our histories and lifestyles, but rather reflect, compare, and contrast attributes of diverse cultures. We can also go about the business of creating viable third spaces for our current societies so that those who live during these uncertain times are better prepared to meet the needs of ever-changing future generations.

Works Cited

Abraham, S. (2014). A nepantla pedagogy: Comparing Anzaldúa's and Bakhtin's ideas for pedagogical and social change. *Critical Education*, 5(5). http://ojs.library.ubc.ca/index.php/criticaled/article/view/183601.
Alexander, R. (2009a). Border crossings: Toward a comparative pedagogy. *Comparative Education*, 37(4), 507–523.
Alexander, R. (2009b). Towards a comparative pedagogy. In R. Cowen & A. M. Kazamias (Eds.), *International handbook of comparative education* (pp. 923–942). New York: Springer.
Alexander, R. (2018a). Developing dialogic teaching: Genesis, process, trial. *Research Papers in Education*. https://doi.org/10.1080/02671522.2018.1481140.
Alexander, R. (2018b). *Dialogic teaching in brief*. https://www.robinalexander.org.uk/wp-content/uploads/2012/10/Dialogc-teaching-in-brief-170622.pdf.
Alleman, J., & Brophy, J. (2010). Effective integration of social studies and literacy. In M. E. McGuire & C. Bronwyn (Eds.), *Making a difference: Revitalizing elementary social studies* (pp. 51–66). Silver Spring, MD: National Council for the Social Studies.
Amigó, M. F. (2017). Confronting school: Immigrant families, hope, education. *Diaspora, Indigenous, and Minority Education*, 11(3), 148–161. https://doi.org/10.1080/15595692.2016.1238356.
Anzaldúa, G. (1987). *Borderlands/La frontera: The new mestiza*. San Francisco, CA: Aunt Lute Books.
Anzaldúa, G. (2002). Now let us shift… the path of conocimiento… inner work public acts. In G. Anzaldúa & A. Keating (Eds.), *This bridge we call home: Radical visions for transformation* (pp. 540–577). New York: Routledge.
Apple, M. W. (2004). *Ideology and curriculum* (3rd ed.). New York: Routledge.
Bakhtin, M. M. (1981). *The dialogic imagination* (C. Emerson & M. Holquist, trans.). Austin, TX: University of Texas Press. (original work published 1975).
Bakhtin, M. M., Holquist, M., & Liapunov, V. (1993). *Toward a philosophy of the act*. Austin: University of Texas Press.

Banks, J. (2009). Multicultural education: Theoretical perspectives and issues. In J. Banks (Ed.), *The Routledge international companion to multicultural education* (pp. 9–32). New York: Routledge.

Barnhardt, R. (2008). Creating a place for indigenous knowledge in education: The Alaska native knowledge network. In D. Gruenewald & G. Smith (Eds.), *Place-based education in the global age: local diversity* (pp. 113–133). Hillsdale, NJ: Lawrence Erlbaum Associates.

Beck, U. (2009). Cosmopolitanization without cosmopolitans: On the distinction between normative and empirical-analytical cosmopolitanism in philosophy and the social sciences. In K. Ikas & G. Wagner (Eds.), *Communicating in the third space* (pp.11–25). New York: Routledge.

Beck-Gernsheim, E., Butler, J., & Puigvert, L. (2003). *Women and social transformation.* Lanham, MD: Rowman & Littlefield.

Bereday, G. Z. (1964). *Comparative method in education [by] George Z. F. Bereday.* New York: Holt Rinehart and Winston.

Berg, J. (2020). A month after George Floyd's death, the hard work begins in Minneapolis, St. Paul. *USA Today*, July 25, 2020. https://www.usatoday.com/story/news/nation/2020/06/25/month-after-george-floyds-death-what-next-minneapolis-st-paul/3198209001/.

Bhabha, H. K. (2004). *The location of culture.* London: Routledge.

Bhabha, H. K. (2009). In the cave of making; thoughts on third space. In K. Ikas & G. Wagner (Eds.), *Communicating in the third space.* New York: Routledge.

Birnbaum, M. (2020). Europe said U. S. influence had waned under Trump. Then Black Lives Matter protests rocked the continent. *Washington Post*, July 22, 2020. https://www.washingtonpost.com/world/europe/europe-said-us-influence-had-waned-under-trump-then-black-lives-matter-protests-rocked-the-continent/2020/06/17/23f88ff2-ab4c-11ea-a43b-be9f6494a87d_story.html.

Bourdieu, P. (1977). Cultural reproduction and social reproduction. In J. Karabel & A. H. Halsey (Eds.), *Power and ideology in education* (pp. 487–511). Oxford, UK: Oxford University Press.

Bowers, C. A. (2008). Why a critical pedagogy of place is an oxymoron. *Environmental Education Research*, *14*(3), 325–335. https://doi.org/10.1080/13504620802156470.

Bowles, S., & Gintis, H. (1976). *Schooling in capitalist America: Educational reform and the contradictions of economic life.* New York: Basic Books.

Bowles, S., & Gintis, H. (2011). *Schooling in capitalist America: Educational reform and the contradictions of economic life.* Chicago, IL: Haymarket Books.

Brandist, C. (1996). Bakhtin, Gramsci, and the semiotics of hegemony. *New Left Review*, *1*(216). http://www.reocities.com/ Athens/aegean/6450/hegemony.htm.

Breuing, M. (2011). Problematizing critical pedagogy. *International Journal of Critical Pedagogy*, *3*(3), 2–23.

Brock, L., Geis, A., & Muller, H. (2006). Introduction: The theoretical challenge of democratic wars. In A. Geis, L. Brock, & H. Muller (Eds.), *Democratic wars: Looking at the dark side of democratic peace* (pp. 3–12). Basingstoke, UK: Palgrave Macmillan.

Carlson, R. (2005). The question concerning curriculum theory. *Journal of the American Association for Advancement of Curriculum Studies* (1).

Carnoy, M., Gove, A. K., & Marshall, J. H. (2007). *Cuba's academic advantage: Why students in Cuba do better in school*. Palo Alto, CA: Stanford University Press.

Cashman, T. G. (2005). Students and their local history projects in a Southwestern United States classroom. *Journal of Border Educational Research, 4*(2), 41–46.

Cashman, T. G. (2013). Border pedagogy as a conduit: Comparing the perspectives of educators in Malaysia, Mexico, and Canada. *Multicultural Education, 20*(2), 2–9.

Cashman, T. G. (2015). *Developing critical border dialogism: Learning from fellow educators in Malaysia, Mexico, Canada, and the United States*. Charlotte, NC: Information Age.

Cashman, T. G. (2016a). Critical border praxis: Choosing the path of critical border dialogism. *Critical Education, 7*(1), 1–16.

Cashman, T. G. (2016b). Navigating the intersection of place-based pedagogy and border pedagogy: Resituating our positions through dialogic understandings. *International Journal of Critical Pedagogy, 7*(1), 29–50.

Cashman, T. G. (2019). "In spite of the way the world is": What United States educators can learn from their counterparts in Cuba. *International Journal of Comparative Education and Development, 22*(1), 16–29. https://doi.org/10.1108/IJCED-11-2018-0050.

Cashman, T. G., & McDermott, B. (2011). From a mouse to an elephant: Canadian teachers, students, and their perspectives of US policies in the curriculum. *Research in Comparative and International Education, 6*, 161–169.

Cashman, T. G., & McDermott, B. (2013). International issues, high stakes testing, and border pedagogy: Social studies at Border High School. *Issues in Teacher Education, 22*(2), 55–68.

Cervantes-Soon, C. G. (2012). *Testimonios* of life and learning in the borderlands: Subaltern Ju´arez girls speak. *Equity & Excellence in Education, 45*(3), 373–391. https://doi.org/10.1080/10665684.2012.698182.

Clark, K., & Holquist, M. (1984). *Mikhail Bakhtin*. Cambridge, MA: Belknap Press of Harvard University Press.

Cline, Z., & Necochea, J. (2003). Education in the borderlands: A border pedagogy conceptual model. *El Bordo: Retos de Frontera, 6*(11), 43–52.

Cohen, J. (1996). *For love of country: Debating the limits of patriotism*. Chicago, IL: University of Chicago Press.

Common Core State Standards Initiative. (2020). http://www.corestandards.org/.

Creswell, J. W. (2013). *Qualitative inquiry & research design: Choosing among five approaches* (3rd ed.). Thousand Oaks, CA: SAGE.

Daase, C. (2006). Democratic war. Three reasons why democracies are war-prone. In A. Geis, L. Brock, & H. Muller (Eds.), *Democratic wars: Looking at the dark side of democratic peace* (pp. 74–89). Basingstoke, UK: Palgrave Macmillan.

Danovich, T. (2017). *The Foxfire book series that preserved Appalachian foodways*. https://www.npr.org/sections/thesalt/2017/03/17/520038859/the-foxfire-book-series-that-preserved-appalachian-foodways.

Darling-Hammond, L., & McCloskey, L. (2011). Assessment for learning around the world: What would it mean to be internationally competitive? In A. C. Ornstein, E. F. Pajak, & S. B. Ornstein (Eds.), *Contemporary issues in curriculum* (2nd ed., pp. 336–347). Upper Saddle River, NJ: Pearson.

Davis, O. L., Jr. (2005). Where is the Iraq war in the curriculum this year? Or is it missing? *Journal of Curriculum and Supervision, 20*(3), 183–187.

DeBotton, L., Puigvert, L., & Sánchez, M. (2005). *The inclusion of other women: Breaking the silence through dialogic learning.* Dordrecht: Springer.

Delanty, G. (2006). The cosmopolitan imagination: Critical cosmopolitanism and social theory. *British Journal of Sociology, 57*(1), 25–47.

Delgado Bernal, D., Aleman, E., & Garavito, A. (2009). Latina/o undergraduate students mentoring Latina/o elementary students: A borderlands analysis of shifting identities and first-year experiences. *Harvard Educational Review, 79*, 560–585.

Delgado Bernal, D. B., Burciaga, R., & Flores Carmona, J. (2012). Chicana/Latina testimonios: Mapping the methodological, pedagogical, and political. *Equity & Excellence in Education, 45*(3), 363–372. http://dx.doi.org/10.1080/10665684.2012.698149.

Demarest, A. B. (2014). *Place-based curriculum design.* New York: Routledge.

DePalma, R. (2010). Toward a practice of polyphonic dialogue in multicultural teacher education. *Curriculum Inquiry, 40*(3), 436–453. https://doi.org/10.1111/j.1467-873X.2010.00492.x.

Dewey, J. (1910). *How we think.* D. C. Heath. https://doi.org/10.1037/10903-000.

Dewey, J. (1959). School and society. In M. Dworkin (Ed.), *Dewey on education* (pp. 76–78). New York: Teachers College Press.

Dimitriadis, G., & Kamberelis, G. (2006). *Theory for education.* New York, NY: Routledge.

Easton, L., & Hewson, K. (2018). From border pedagogy to treaty pedagogy: Canadian exceptionalism in a Canadian film studies classroom. *Canadian Review of American Studies, 48*, 63–83. https://www.muse.jhu.edu/article/684973.

Elder, J. (1999). In pursuit of a bioregional curriculum: An interview with John Elder. *Orion Afield: Working for Nature and Community, 3*(2), 26–28.

Emekauwa, E. (2004). The star with my name: The Alaska Rural Systemic Initiative and the impact of place-based education on Native student achievement. In D. T. Williams (Ed.), *Rural trust white paper on place-based education.* Arlington, VA: Rural School and Community Trust.

Epstein, E. H. (2008). Setting the normative boundaries: Crucial epistemological benchmarks in comparative education. *Comparative Education, 44*(4), 373–386. http://dx.doi.org/10.1080/03050060802481405.

Fischer, B., & Peters, Z. (2016). Cashing in on kids: 172 ALEC education bills push privatization in 2015. *PR Watch.* https://www.prwatch.org/news/2016/03/13054/cashing-kids-172-alec-education-bills-2015#:~:text=ALEC's%20education%20task%20force%20has,unions%2C%20and%20lower%20teaching%20standards.&text=ALEC%20model%20bills%20divert%20taxpayer,%22tuition%20tax%20credit%22%20programs.

Flinders, D. J. (2006). We can and should teach the war in Iraq. *Educational Digest, 71*(5), 8–12.

Flores, B. B., & Clark, E. R. (2002). *El desarrollo del proyecto alianza: Lessons learned and policy implications*. Tempe, AZ: Arizona State University, Southwest Center for Educational Equity and Language Diversity.

Foxfire. (2019). *About Foxfire*. December 11, 2019. https://www.foxfire.org/about-foxfire/.

Freire, P. (1995). *Pedagogy of hope: Reliving pedagogy of the oppressed*. New York: Continuum.

Freire, P. (2005). *Pedagogy of the oppressed* (30th anniversary ed.). Continuum: New York.

Fuentes, C. M., & Peña, S. (2010). Globalization, transborder networks, and U.S.-Mexico border cities. In K. Staudt, C. Fuentes, & J. Monárrez Fragoso (Eds.), *Cities and citizenship at the U.S.-Mexico border* (pp. 1–20). New York: Palgrave Macmillan.

Garii, B. (2014). Cuban/US boundaries: The unspoken socio-political contexts of research agendas. In S. Sharma, J. Phillion, J. Rahatzad, & H. L. Sasser (Eds.), *Internationalizing teacher education for social justice: Theory, research, and practice* (pp. 163–177). Charlotte, NC: Information Age.

Garza, E. (2007). Becoming a border pedagogy educator: Rooting practice in paradox. *Multicultural Education, 15*(1), 2–7.

Giroux, H. A. (1988a). Border pedagogy in the age of postmodernism. *Journal of Education, 170*(3), 162–181.

Giroux, H. A. (1988b). *Teachers as intellectuals: Toward a critical pedagogy of learning*. Westport, CT: Bergin & Garvey.

Giroux, H. A. (1991). Border pedagogy and the politics of postmodernism. *Social Text, 28*, 51–67.

Giroux, H. A. (2005). *Border crossings: Cultural workers and the politics of education* (2nd ed.). New York: Routledge.

Glenn, C. L. (2007). Common problems, different solutions. *Peabody Journal of Education, 82*(2–3), 530–548.

Glesne, C. (2011). *Becoming qualitative researchers: An introduction*. Boston: Pearson.

Goldstein, D., Popescu, A., & Hannah-Jones, N. (2020). As school moves online, many students stay logged out. *New York Times*, April 7, 2020. https://www.msn.com/en-us/news/us/as-school-moves-online-many-students-stay-logged-out/ar-BB12dv8p?li=BBnb7Kz.

González, N., Moll, L. C., & Amanti, C. (Eds.). (2005). *Funds of knowledge: Theorizing practices in households, communities, and classrooms*. Lawrence Erlbaum Associates Publishers.

Goodrick, D. (2014). *Comparative case studies, methodological briefs: Impact evaluation 9*. Florence, IT: UNICEF Office of Research.

Gore, J. M. (1993). *The struggle for pedagogies*. New York: Routledge.

Gramsci, A. (1971). *Selections from the prison notebooks of Antonio Gramsci* (Eds. Q. Hoare & G. Nowell-Smith). New York: International Publishers.

Grande, S. (2015). *Red pedagogy: Native American social and political thought*. Lanham, MD: Rowman and Littlefield.

Greeley, B., & Fitzgerald, A. (2011). Psst...wanna buy a law? *Bloomberg Businessweek*, June 21, 2020. https://www.bloomberg.com/news/articles/2011-12-01/pssst-dot-w anna-buy-a-law.

Greenwood, D. (2013). A critical theory of place-conscious education. In R. Stevenson, M. Brody, J. Dillon, & A. Wals (Eds.), *International handbook of research on environmental education* (pp. 93–100). New York: Routledge.

Gruenewald, D. A. (2003a). The best of both worlds: A critical pedagogy of place. *Educational Researcher, 32*(4), 3–12.

Gruenewald, D. A. (2003b). Foundations of place: A multidisciplinary framework for place-conscious education. *American Educational Research Journal, 40*(3), 619–654. https://doi.org/10.3102/00028312040003619.

Hage, G. (1998). *White nation: Fantasies of white supremacy in a multicultural society*. Sydney, Australia: Pluto Press.

Halasek, K. (1992). Feminism and Bakhtin: Dialogic reading in the academy. *Rhetoric Society Quarterly, 22*(1), 63–73. June 30, 2020. www.jstor.org/stable/3885655.

Halls, W. D. (1990). *Comparative education: Contemporary issues and trends*. London: J. Kingsley Publishers.

Hampton, E., Liguori, O., & Rippberger, S. (2003). Binational border collaboration in teacher education. *Multicultural Education, 11*(1), 2–10.

Hansen, D. T., Burdick-Shepherd, S., Cammarano, C., & Obelleiro, G. (2009). Education, values, and valuing in cosmopolitan perspective. *Curriculum Inquiry, 39*(5), 587–612.

Holquist, M. (1981). Introduction. In M. Bakhtin (Ed.), *The dialogic imagination: Four essays*. (M. Holquist & C. Emerson, Trans.) Austin, TX: University of Texas Press. (Original work published in 1975).

Holquist, M. (2002). *Dialogism: Bakhtin and his world* (2nd ed.). New York: Routledge.

Holt, J. (1989). *Learning all the time*. New York: Addison-Wesley.

hooks, B. (2014). *Teaching to transgress*. New York: Routledge.

Isik-Ercan, Z. (2014). Third spaces: Turkish immigrants and their children at the intersection of identity, schooling, and culture. *Diaspora, Indigenous, and Minority Education, 8*(3), 127–144. https://doi.org/10.1080/15595692.2014.897222.

James, W. (1906). *What pragmatism means*. http://www.marxists.org/reference/s ubject/philosophy/works/us/james.htm.

Kasanjian, C. J. (2011). The border pedagogy revisited. *Intercultural Education, 22*(5), 371–380. https://doi.org/10.1080/14675986.2011.643135.

Kincheloe, J. L. (2008). Critical pedagogy and the knowledge wars of the twenty-first century. *International Journal of Critical Pedagogy, 1*(1), 1–22.

Kleingeld, P., & Brown, E. (2006). Cosmopolitanism. In E. N. Zalta (Ed.), *Stanford encyclopedia of philosophy*. Stanford, CA. July 1, 2020. http://plato.stanford.edu/entries/cosmopolitanism/.

Kliebard, H. M. (2004). *The struggle for the American curriculum, 1893–1958*. New York, NY: Routledge Falmer.

Kolossov, V., & Scott, J. (2013). Selected conceptual issues in border studies. *Belgeo, 1*. http://belgeo.revues.org/10532.

Koopman, C. (2006). Pragmatism as a philosophy of hope: Emerson, James, Dewey, and Rorty. *Journal of Speculative Philosophy, 20*(2), 106–116.

Kozol, J. (1978). A new look at the literacy campaign in Cuba. *Harvard Educational Review, 48*, 341–377.

Lam, S. G. (2016). From Rabun county to Yonji county. In H. Smith & J. C. McDermott (Eds.), *The Foxfire approach* (pp. 73–82). Rotterdam, NL: Sense Publishers.

Lather, P. (1998). Critical pedagogy and its complicities: A praxis of stuck places. *Educational Theory, 48*(4), 487–497.

Lather, P. (2001). Postbook: Working the ruins of feminist ethnography. *Signs, 27*(1), 199–227.

Latina Feminist Group (2001). *Telling to live: Latina feminist testimonios*. Durham, NC: Duke University Press.

Lefebvre, H. (1991). *The production of space* (D. Nicholson-Smith, Trans.). Malden, MA: Blackwell Publishing.

Lefebvre, H., Nicholson-Smith, D., & Harvey, D. (1991). *The production of space*. Oxford, UK: Blackwell Publishing.

Leonardo, Z. (2004). Critical social theory and transformative knowledge: The functions of criticism in quality education. *Educational Researcher, 33*(11), 11–18. https://doi.org/10.3102/0013189X033006011.

Leon-Guerrero, A., Kelleher, A., & O'Connell Killen, P. (2019). Documenting community dialogue's practice and projected outcomes. Paper presented on July 29, 2019 at Pacific Lutheran University, Tacoma, WA.

Liddicoat, A. J. (2009). Evolving ideologies of the intercultural in Australian multicultural and language education policy. *Journal of Multilingual and Multicultural Development, 30*(3), 189–203. https://doi.org/10.1080/01434630802369429.

Lindaman, D., & Ward, K. (2004). *History lessons: How textbooks from around the world portray U.S. history*. New York: The New Press.

Lizárraga, J. R., & Gutiérrez, K. D. (2018). Centering nepantla literacies from the borderlands: Leveraging "in-betweenness" toward learning in the everyday. *Theory into Practice, 57*(1), 38–47. https://doi.org/10.1080/00405841.2017.1392164.

Lu, C. (2000). The one and many faces of cosmopolitanism. *The Journal of Political Philosophy, 8*(2): 244–267.

Lutjens, S. L. (2007). (Re)reading Cuban educational policy: Schooling and the third revolution. In I. Epstein (Ed.), *Recapturing the personal: Essays on education and embodied knowledge in comparative perspective* (pp. 163–194). Greenwich, CT: Information Age Publishing.

Maffie, J. (2007). The centrality of nepantla in conquest-era Nahua philosophy. *Nahua Newsletter, 44*, 11–22. http://www.nahuanewsletter.org/nnarchive/newsletters/Nahua44.pdf.

Martínez, O. (1994). *Border people: Live and society in the U.S.-Mexico borderlands*. Tucson, AZ: University of Arizona Press.

Matusov, E. (2009). *Journey into dialogic pedagogy*. Hauppauge, NY: Nova Science Publishers.

Menchu, R. (1984). *I, Rigoberta Menchu. An Indian woman in Guatemala* (E. Burgos-Debray, Ed., A. Wright, Trans.). London, England: Verso.

Meredith, P. (1998, July 7–9). Hybridity in the third space: Rethinking bi-cultural politics in Aotearoa/New Zealand. Paper presented to Te Oru Rangahau Maori Research and Development Conference, Massey University. http://lianz.waikato.ac.nz/PAPERS/paul/hybridity.pdf.

Mignolo, W. D. (2000a). Introduction: From cross-genealogies and subaltern knowledges to nepantla. *Nepantla: Views from South, 1*(1), 1–8.

Mignolo, W. D. (2000b). The many faces of cosmo-polis: Border thinking and critical cosmopolitanism. *Public Culture, 12*(3), 721–748.

Mignolo, W. (2012). *Local histories/global designs: Coloniality, subaltern knowledges, and border thinking*. Princeton, NJ: Princeton University Press.

Mohanty, C. T. (2003). "Under western eyes" revisited: Feminist solidarity through anticapitalist struggles. In C. T. Mohanty (Ed.), *Feminism without borders: Decolonizing theory, practicing solidarity* (pp. 221–251). Durham, NC: Duke University Press.

Mora, P. (2008). *Nepantla: Essays from the land in the middle*. Albuquerque, NM: University of New Mexico Press.

Necochea, J., & Cline, Z. (2005). Borderland education and teacher education reform in California: Unfulfilled promises. *Journal of Borderlands Studies, 20*(1), 129–141.

Nelles, W. (2003a). *Comparative education, terrorism and human security: From critical pedagogy to peacekeeping*. New York: Palgrave MacMillan.

Nelles, W. (2003b). Conclusions: Toward a new critical pedagogy in the shadow of perpetual war. In W. Nelles (Ed.), *Comparative education, terrorism, and human security* (pp. 237–256). New York: Palgrave Macmillan.

New American Economy. (2019). Understanding the impact of refugee resettlement in the United States: Data analysis, stories, and resources for lesson planning. *Social Education, 83*(6), 330–335.

New Mexico Public Education Department. (2018). *New Mexico national school lunch program*. https://webnew.ped.state.nm.us/wp-content/uploads/2018/02/October-Free-Reduced-Lunch-Data-Report-SY-17-18.pdf.

Nolan, C., & Stitzlein, S. M. (2011). Meaningful hope for teachers in times of high anxiety and low morale. *Democracy and Education, 19*(1), 1–11.

Ornstein. A. C. (2011). Philosophy as a basis for curriculum decisions. In A C. Orstein, E. F. Pajak, & S. B. Ornstein (Eds.), *Contemporary issues in curriculum* (5th ed., pp. 2–9). Boston: Pearson.

Paasi, A. (2011). A *border theory*: An unattainable dream or a realistic aim for border scholars? In D. Wastl-Walter (Ed.), *The Ashgate research companion to border studies*. London: Ashgate.

Phillips, D., & Schweisfurth, M. (2006). *Comparative and international education: An introduction to theory, method, and practice*. London, UK: Continuum.

Pinar, W. F. (2011). *What is curriculum theory?* (2nd ed.). New York: Routledge.

Prieto, L., & Villenas, S. A. (2012). Pedagogies from nepantla: Testimonio, Chicana/Latina feminisms and teacher education classrooms. *Equity & Excellence in Education, 45*(3), 411–429. https://doi.org/10.1080/10665684.2012.698197.

Puigvert, L. (2012). The dialogic turn: Dialogue or violence? *International and Multidisciplinary Journal of Social Sciences*, *1*(1), 78–96. https://doi.org/10.4471/rimcis.2012.04.

Raffan, J. (1992). *Frontier, homeland and sacred space: A collaborative investigation into cross-cultural perceptions of place in the Thelon Game Sanctuary, Northwest Territories*. Unpublished doctoral dissertation, Kingston, ON: Queens University.

Ramirez, P. C., Ross, L., & Jimenez-Silva, M. (2016). The intersectionality of border pedagogy and Latino/a youth: Enacting border pedagogy in multiple spaces. *The High School Journal*, *99*(4), 302–321.

Rapaport, A. (2020). Global pandemic: A painful lesson for social studies educators. *Journal of International Social Studies*, *10*(1), 1–2.

Reilly, N. (2011). Doing transnational feminism, transforming human rights: The emancipatory possibilities revisited. *Irish Journal of Sociology*, *19*(2), 60–76. https://doi.org/10.7227/IJS.19.2.5.

Reyes, M. D. L. (2005). Introduction to the special issue: Educational lives on the border. *Journal of Latinos and Education*, *4*(3), 149–152.

Reyes, M. D. L., & Garza, E. (2005). Teachers on the border: In their own words. *Journal of Latinos and Education*, *4*(3), 153–170.

Reza-Lopez, E., Huera-Charles, L., & Reyes, L. V. (2014). Nepantlera pedagogy: An axiological posture for preparing critically conscious teachers in the Borderlands. *Journal of Latinos in Education*, *13*(2), 107–119.

Román-Odio, C. (2013). Nepantlismo, Chicana approach to colonial ideology. In *Sacred iconographies in Chicana cultural productions: Comparative feminist studies series* (pp. 51–74). New York: Palgrave Macmillan.

Romo, J. J., & Chavez, C. (2006). Border pedagogy: A study of pre-service teacher transformation. *The Educational Forum*, *70*, 142–153.

Rorty, R. (1999). *Philosophy and social hope*. New York: Penguin Books.

Rosenberg, M. (2020, February 20). Trump's 'remain in Mexico' immigration policy allowed to proceed temporarily. *Reuters*. https://www.reuters.com/article/us-usa-immigration-mexico/trumps-remain-in-mexico-immigration-policy-allowed-to-proceed-temporarily-idUSKCN20M2SC.

Rothstein, R. (2015, April 3). Taking the fall in Atlanta. *Economic Policy Institute*. https://www.epi.org/blog/taking-the-fall-in-atlanta/.

Salinas, C., Vickery, A., & Franquiz, M. (2016). Advancing border pedagogies: Understandings of citizenship through comparisons of home to school contexts. *The High School Journal*, *99*(4), 322–336. http://www.jstor.org/stable/44075303.

Schulze-Engler, F. (2009). Transcultural negotiations: Third spaces in modern times. In K. Ikas & G. Wagner (Eds.), *Communicating in the third space* (pp. 149–168). New York: Routledge.

Shade, P. (2001). *Habits of hope: A pragmatic theory*. Nashville, TN: Vanderbilt University Press.

Shade, P. (2006). Educating hopes. *Studies in Philosophy and Education*, *25*, 191–225. https://doi.org/10.1007/s11217-005-1251-2.

Shapiro, A. (2016). In the mountains of Georgia, Foxfire students keep Appalachian culture alive, November 3, 2016. *All Things Considered*, December 11, 2019.

https://www.npr.org/2016/11/03/500279267/in-the-mountains-of-georgia-foxfire-students-keep-appalachian-culture-alive.

Sharing Our Pathways, A Newsletter of the Alaska Rural Systemic Initiative. (2000, September/October). *5*(4), June 30, 2020. http://ankn.uaf.edu/sop/sopv5i4.html.

Shear, S. B., Tschida, C. M., Bellows, E., Buchanan, L. B., & Saylor, E. E. (2018). *(Re)imagining elementary social studies: A controversial issues reader.* Charlotte, NC: Information Age Publishing.

Smets, F. (2019). Why we need to teach about refugees. *Social Education, 83*(6), 311–316.

Smith, G. A. (2002). Place-based education: Learning to be where we are. *Phi Delta Kappan, 83*(8), 584–594. https://doi.org/10.1177/003172170208300806.

Smith, G. A. (2016). The past, present, and future of place-based learning. *Getting Smart*, December 11, 2019. https://www.gettingsmart.com/2016/11/past-present-and-future-of-place-based-learning/.

Smith, G. A., & Sobel, D. (2010). *Place- and community-based education in schools.* New York: Routledge.

Smith, L. T. (2005). *Decolonizing methodologies: Research and indigenous peoples.* New York, NY: Zed Books.

Sobel, D. (2005). *Place-based education: Connecting classrooms and communities* (2nd ed.). Great Barrington, MA: Orion Society.

Social Studies Standards Grades 5–8. (2008). https://webnew.ped.state.nm.us/wp-content/uploads/2018/01/SocialStudiesStandards_5-8.pdf.

Soja, E. W. (2009). Thirdspace; toward a new consciousness of space and spatiality. In K. Ikas & G. Wagner (Eds.), *Communicating in the third space* (pp. 45–61). New York: Routledge.

Stake, R. E. (2000). Case studies. In N. K. Denzin & Y. S. Lincoln (Eds.), *Handbook of qualitative research* (2nd ed., pp. 435–454). Thousand Oaks, CA: Sage Publications, Inc.

Stanger, C. (2018). From critical education to an embodied pedagogy of hope: Seeking a liberatory praxis with Black, working class girls in the neoliberal 16–19 college. *Studies in Philosophy and Education, 37*, 47–63. https://doi.org/10.1007/s11217-016-9561-0.

Starnes, B., Paris, C., & Stevens, C. (1999). *The Foxfire core practices: Discussions and implications.* Mountain City, GA: Foxfire.

Staudt, K., & Spener, D. (1998). The view from the frontier: Theoretical perspectives undisciplined. In D. Spener & K. Staudt (Eds.), *The U.S.-Mexico border: Transcending divisions, contesting identities* (pp. 3–33). Boulder, CO: Lynne Rienner.

Stitzlein, S. M. (2019). *Learning how to hope: Reviving democracy through schools and civil society.* New York: Oxford University Press.

Supko, R. (1998). *Perspectives on the Cuban national literacy campaign.* Latin American Studies Association Conference, Chicago, Illinois, September 24–26.

Tam, G., & El-Azar, D. (2020). Three ways the coronavirus pandemic could reshape education. *World Education Forum.* https://www.weforum.org/agenda/2020/03/3-ways-coronavirus-is-reshaping-education-and-what-changes-might-be-here-to-stay/.

Tan, K. C. (2004). *Justice without borders: Cosmopolitanism, nationalism and patriotism*. Cambridge: Cambridge University Press.

Tatto, M. T. (2011). Reimagining the education of teachers: The role of comparative and international research. *Comparative Education Review, 55*(4), 495–516.

Tibbitts, F., & Katz, S. (2018). Dilemmas and hopes for human rights education: Curriculum and learning in international contexts. *Prospects: Quarterly Review of Comparative Education, 47*(1–2), 31–40.

United States Department of State, Bureau of Consular Affairs. (2018). *Cuba sanctions*. August 22, 2018. https://www.treasury.gov/resourcecenter/sanctions/Programs/Pages/cuba.aspx.

Valencia, R. R., & Black, M. S. (2002). "Mexican Americans don't value education!" On the basis of the myth, mythmaking, and debunking. *Journal of Latinos and Education, 1*(2), 81–103.

Valenzuela, A. (1999). *Subtractive schooling: U.S.-Mexican youth and the politics of caring*. Albany, NY: State University of New York Press.

Vertovec, S., & Cohen, R. (2002). *Conceiving cosmopolitanism*. Oxford, UK: Oxford University Press.

Vygotsky, L. (1962). *Studies in communication: Thought and language* (E. Hanfmann & G. Vakar, Eds.). MIT Press. https://doi.org/10.1037/11193-000.

Wattchow, B., & Brown, M. (2011). *A pedagogy of place*. Victoria, AU: Monash University Publishing.

Wigginton, E. (1991). Culture begins at home. *Educational Leadership, 49*(4), 60–64.

Wilson, D. A. (2003). The future of international and comparative education in a globalised world. In M. Bray (Ed.), *Comparative education: Continuing traditions, new challenges, and new paradigms* (pp. 15–33). Dordrecht, The Netherlands: Kluwer Academic Publishers.

Yaeger, P. (1991). Afterward. In D. M. Bauer & S. J. McKinstry (Eds.), *Feminism, Bakhtin, and the dialogic* (pp 239–245). Albany, NY: State University of New York Press.

Yin, R. K. (2003). *Case study research: Design and methods*. Thousand Oaks, CA: Sage Publications.

Yuval-Davis, N. (2006). Human/women's rights and feminist transversal polities. In M. M. Ferree & A. M. Tripp (Eds.), *Global feminism: Women's transnational activism, organizing, and human rights* (pp. 275–294). New York: New York University Press.

Index

Abraham, Stephanie, 32–36, 50, 54, 57, 77, 91
Alaska place-based education, 19, 22–23, 25
Alexander, Robin J., 50, 63, 119–23
American Legislative Exchange Council (ALEC), 146–47
Amigó, Maria Florencia, 128–29
anti-terrorism, 2, 75
Anzaldúa, Gloria, 3, 4, 10, 29, 32–36, 50, 57, 77, 90, 91, 129
Apple, Michael, 49, 67

Bakhtin, Mikhail, 3, 4, 29, 31–34, 36, 39, 50, 53–55, 77, 91, 120
Bereday, George, 121, 123
Bhabha, Homi, 88, 93, 129, 135–38
Black Lives Matter, 142, 151
border crossings, 1, 3, 5, 12, 63, 90, 129, 135
border pedagogy, 2–5, 7–15, 17, 49–62, 64–65, 67, 71, 73, 75, 76, 85, 87, 90, 91, 95, 104–5, 112, 116, 118, 124; democratic education and, 9, 24, 51, 64; US/Canada contexts of, 2, 7, 12–14, 74, 80, 82, 127–28; US/Cuba contexts of, 87–102; US/Mexico contexts of, 10–14, 65, 81–82, 103–6, 115, 117, 126–27, 138

Bourdieu, Pierre, 60, 68, 83
Bowles, Samuel and Gintis, Herbert, 50, 60, 68, 77, 83
Boy in the Striped Pajamas, 113, 116

Canada, 2, 3, 5, 7, 12–14, 21, 73–75, 79, 80, 82, 127–29; Ontario case study, 2, 13, 74–75, 78–79, 82
Carter, Melvin, 143–44
Cashman, Timothy G., 3, 10, 13, 14, 23, 31, 49, 76, 77, 85, 88, 90, 100, 104, 105, 116
Center for Media and Democracy, 146
Cervantes-Soon, Claudia, 40, 90, 100, 126
Charlottesville, Virginia, 7
China, 21, 24–25, 131; place-based education in, 21, 24–25
collectivism, 122, 151
Community Dialogue (CD), 132–33
comparative education, 74, 96, 99, 121–26
comparative pedagogy, 122–23
conflict resolution, 6, 15, 59, 68–70, 88, 131, 139, 143
Core Curriculum, 114
correspondence principle, 50, 60, 68, 77, 83
cosmopolitanism, 43–45, 90, 91, 93, 150

COVID-19, 1, 7, 27, 103, 118, 142, 145, 147–51
Creswell, John W., 78, 95, 105, 106
critical border dialogism, 2, 3, 5, 49–63, 65–72, 76, 77, 83, 87, 88, 90, 91
critical border praxis, 2, 3, 5, 6, 31, 53, 57, 62–73, 77, 83, 84, 87, 88, 93, 100, 102, 103, 119, 134, 143, 149–51
critical cosmopolitanism, 2–5, 43–50, 53, 55–57, 65, 67, 77, 90, 91, 101, 134, 141, 148, 150
critical pedagogy of place, 5, 19, 20, 26, 51, 52, 64, 75, 76, 90, 91
cross-comparative research, 5, 73, 79
Cuba, 5, 7, 14, 87–103, 106, 111, 114, 115; Cuban literacy campaign, 89, 90, 94; educational policy, 14, 89; educators, 5, 14, 87, 88, 91, 93, 94, 97–100, 102
Cuban revolution, 90, 96, 99, 100, 114
Cubation, 96
cultural reproduction, 68, 83
currere, 65–66, 72

Daase, Christopher, 69, 133, 134
Delanty, Gerard, 43–46, 56, 77, 91
Developing a Critical Border Dialogism, 2, 3
Dewey, John, 3, 18, 47, 60
dialogic feminism, 2–5, 29, 38–40, 42, 50, 53, 58, 59, 61, 65, 67, 70, 77, 83, 90, 91, 93, 134, 141, 148, 150
dialogic processes, 1, 2, 6, 31, 59, 63, 131–33, 135, 139, 151
disinformation, 1, 151
diversality, 56–57, 120, 121

El Paso, Texas mass shooting, 7
Esperanza Rising, 112

Foxfire, 18–19, 22–24
Freire, Paolo, 3, 19, 48, 67, 77, 89–90, 93, 124, 134
Frey, Jacob, 143–44

Giroux, Henry, 3, 8–10, 51, 64–65, 76, 78, 90, 95, 104, 105
Glesne, Corrine, 95, 106
globalization, 5, 39, 41, 43, 45, 46, 56, 77, 91, 150
global pandemic, 142, 144
Gore, Jennifer, 39
Gramsci, Antonio, 2, 3, 53, 54, 67
Grande, Sandy, 37–39, 57–58, 91, 93; Grande's red pedagogy, 37, 57, 58
Gruenewald, David, 3, 19–20, 26, 51, 64, 75, 90

heteroglossia, 2–5, 29–33, 38, 50, 53–55, 65, 67, 77, 90, 91, 134, 141, 148, 149
House on Mango Street, 112
human rights education (HRE), 134
hybridity, 45, 93, 135, 138, 149

immigration, 6–7, 82, 103, 106, 107, 109, 111, 112, 114–15, 117, 118, 128; recent immigration from Central America, 57, 104, 106, 111, 113–15
interconnectedness, 11, 27, 44, 56, 61, 83, 91
intersectionality, 4, 5, 20, 26, 29, 39, 41, 42, 49, 50, 52, 58, 65, 67, 73, 97, 118, 135
Iraq War, 2, 67, 73–75, 80–81, 133

James, William, 29, 30, 50, 55, 59, 60, 77, 91

Kincheloe, Joe L., 56, 72
King, Jr., Martin Luther, 97, 100
Kliebard, Herbert M., 30, 50, 55
Koopman, Colin, 30, 46, 50, 55, 60, 77, 91

Lefebvre, Henri, 88, 136, 137
Lincoln, Abraham, 97, 100
Lindaman, Dana and Ward, Kyle, 125, 127–28

Lizárraga, Jose Ramon and Gutiérrez, Kris, 35, 37, 138

Maffie, James, 34, 35, 50, 57, 77, 91, 129
Malaysia, 2, 3, 5, 7, 73–75, 78–81, 103; Malaysian educators, 73–75
Malcolm X, 97
Martí, Jose, 89, 96, 97
meliorism, 2–5, 27, 29–31, 43, 46, 50, 52, 53, 55, 65, 67, 77, 90, 91, 134, 141, 148–51
Mexico, 2–7, 10–12, 14, 29, 33, 34, 57, 65, 73–75, 78–82, 103–7, 111, 115, 117, 126–27, 129, 138; Chihuahua, Mexico, case study, 2, 73, 74, 75, 78
Mignolo, Walter, 4, 29, 33, 34, 50, 56, 57, 77, 91, 93, 119, 120
Minneapolis, Minnesota, 142–44; George Floyd death, 142

Nahua people, 34, 57; Nahuatl language, 4, 29, 33, 34, 57
nationalism, 30, 46, 56, 128, 131
Nelles, Wayne, 66–67, 84
nepantla, 2–5, 29, 33–38, 50, 53, 57–58, 61, 65, 67, 77, 83, 90, 91, 93, 129, 134, 138, 141, 148, 149
New American Economy, 117
Northern Ireland, 132–33, 135
Northern Triangle countries, 104

Organization for Economic Co-operation and Development (OECD), 145
Ornstein, Allan C., 52

patriarchy, 32, 40, 58, 59, 77, 91, 93, 99, 126, 150
Pax Americana, 68–70, 100
Pax Universalis, 68–70, 72, 84, 100, 102
Phillips, David and Schweisfurth, Michele, 74, 123–24
Pinar, William, 65–66

place-based education, 4, 5, 17, 19–27, 51, 52, 64, 75, 76, 90, 91
populism, 6, 131, 146
postcolonialism, 39, 135–38
postmodernism, 124, 136, 137
pragmatic hope, 2–5, 14, 38, 43, 46–50, 53, 59–61, 67, 69, 77, 83, 87, 91, 93, 94, 102, 118, 119, 126, 131, 134, 141, 143, 148, 150, 151
praxis, 1–3, 5, 6, 14, 31, 39, 48, 53, 57, 62, 63, 65, 67–73, 77, 83–85, 87–89, 93, 100, 102, 103, 119, 134, 135, 139, 141, 143, 144, 148–51
Puigvert, Lidia, 29, 38–40, 50, 58, 59, 77, 91, 131, 132

reconstructionist curricula, 50, 52, 53, 77
refugees, 6, 103, 111, 113, 115–18
Reilly, Niamh, 40–42
reinvigoration, 151

Sabah, Malaysia, 2, 73, 74, 78
Shade, Patrick A., 2, 30, 43, 46–48, 50, 59–60, 77, 91; habits of hope, 30, 48
Smith, Gregory A., 17–20, 27
Soja, Edward, 88, 93–94, 136–38
Southwest (United States) place-based education, 18, 23–24
Stake, Robert E., 78, 95, 105
subalterns, 37, 40, 119–21

Tam, Gloria and El-Azar, Diana, 145
terrorism, 2, 66, 67, 75, 79–82, 98, 151
testimonios, 35, 37, 40, 126
third space, 1–3, 5, 6, 34, 35, 93, 94, 100, 102, 129, 131–39, 141, 144, 148, 149, 152
third space theory 93, 135, 136
Toward a Philosophy of the Act, 54, 55
transborder dialogue, 3–6, 27, 29, 46, 48, 61, 63, 69, 83, 87, 102, 103, 119, 124, 131, 142, 144, 150

transnational possibilities, 1–3, 5, 6, 11–15, 17, 40, 41, 43–49, 55, 64, 66, 68, 69, 72–76, 79, 83–85, 88, 93–97, 102, 104, 106, 119, 124, 125, 129, 133, 138, 143, 148–51
treaties, 13, 82, 100, 102, 127, 128; Treaty of Guadalupe-Hidalgo, 127
trialectical, 88
Trump administration, 3, 8, 87, 104
Turner Martí, Lidia, 98

unilateralism, 14, 148
United States/Mexico border, 6, 7, 10–12, 34, 65, 74, 75, 78, 79, 81, 82, 103–39

Valenzuela, Angela, 126

War of 1812, 127, 128

Yin, Robert K., 78, 95

About the Author

Timothy G. Cashman is a professor in the Department of Teacher Education at the University of Texas at El Paso. He received his doctoral degree from Washington State University and his master's degree from the University of New Mexico. Dr. Cashman has conducted empirical studies in Mexico, Malaysia, Canada, and the United States. His academic expertise includes the development of the original theoretical constructs of critical border dialogism and critical border praxis, which follows on the principles of border pedagogy and critical, place-based pedagogies. Cashman has taught curriculum and instruction, social studies education, education for a diverse society, middle school methods, and classroom organization. Previous educational experiences include fifteen years of teaching K-12 in New Mexico, California, and Korea. In 2015, Cashman was the sole author of a book entitled *Developing a Critical Border Dialogism: Learning from Fellow Educators in Malaysia, Mexico, Canada, and the United States* by Information Age Publishing. His research was also featured in the following peer reviewed academic journals: *Multicultural Education, Action in Teacher Education, Journal of Social Studies Research, International Journal of Critical Pedagogy, Critical Education, Journal of Authentic Learning, Research in Comparative and International Education, Issues in Teacher Education,* and the *Journal of International Social Studies*. He has also published book chapters in four different books. Most recently, Cashman has been conducting research with academic colleagues based in both Cuba and Japan.

www.ingramcontent.com/pod-product-compliance
Lightning Source LLC
Chambersburg PA
CBHW020123010526
44115CB00008B/953